OCCUPYING LANGUAGE

OCCUPYING LANGUAGE
The Secret Rendezvous with History and the Present

MARINA SITRIN and
DARIO AZZELLINI

Occupied Media Pamphlet Series | Zuccotti Park Press

BROOKLYN

First Zuccotti Park Press paperback edition
published Autumn 2012

Cover art and design by R. Black

Zuccotti Park Press is a project of Adelante Alliance

Produced by Greg Ruggiero

Special thanks to Joe Nevins and Elizabeth Bell

Archived by the Tamiment Collection at New York University

ISBN: 978-1-884519-09-3

Library of Congress Control Number: 2012935091

Printed in the United States of America

9 8 7 6 5 4 3 2 1

Occupied Media Pamphlet Series | Zuccotti Park Press
405 61 Street | Brooklyn, New York 11220
occupy@adelantealliance.org
www.zuccottiparkpress.com

CONTENTS

PRELUDE

On September 19, 2011, a group of twenty participants in Occupy Wall Street were standing in a circle
in Zuccotti Park discussing what it means to facilitate
an assembly, and what the role of facilitators is and
can be. At one point it was suggested that "our role
is to help create the most horizontal space possible."
In response, a young woman asked, "What does
that mean? Horizontal?" Another young woman
responded, "You know, what they did in Argentina,"
and then another asked what that was.

Later, in a university setting in New York, a discussion was taking place with regard to the Occupy
movements, then two months under way, with
assemblies organized in more than 1,500 towns,
cities and villages in the United States alone. A
young participant in the Occupy movements spoke
of how the assemblies are being organized using
horizontalism. A well-known academic responded
that it was amazing that the creation of horizontalism in Occupy Wall Street had spread so quickly
around the world.

Over the days, weeks and months that have followed, so many conversations and relationships
being developed have been reminding us of the past
twenty years of autonomous creation within movements in Argentina, Mexico, Bolivia and Venezuela, as well as the U.S./European global justice
movement.

And then in Spain and Greece, where we recently traveled to meet with people in the movements, we also found that people are both speaking and organizing in ways very similar to what we have seen in Latin America, yet often without any conscious knowledge of or reference to those movements. At one point we began to wonder if there was a way to share some of these experiences and stories from Latin America, so as to put them in dialogue with the movements in the United States and Europe. Then we met with Greg Ruggiero and decided to create a book for the Occupied Media Pamphlet Series in an attempt to do just that.

—Marina Sitrin and Dario Azzellini

AN INVITATION TO A GLOBAL CONVERSATION

Occupying Language is an open conversation. Through it, we invite you to join us to explore insurgent movements that have been organizing in Latin America over the past twenty years, and to connect key concepts and language from those struggles with what is new and beautiful in the social relations being created by people's movements in the United States today. There are of course many similarities with preceding forms of organization and mobilization, especially with the movement for global justice of the late 1990s and early 2000s. However, we are choosing to ground the discussion in movements and groups that arose from and are comprised of ordinary people, rather than activists.

Language is not neutral, and words transport and express concepts and ways of thinking. They can consolidate and perpetuate hierarchies, domination and control just as they can underline equality and strengthen consciousness. Latin American struggles for dignity, freedom and liberation are rooted in more than five hundred years of resistance. Language derived from their struggles comes with historical antecedents.

In *Occupying Language* we describe the

experiences of the movements from the position of accompanyment, walking together, and thinking together about the many possible meanings of the diverse practices. Throughout this text we share the words and voices of the movement actors themselves, in order to facilitate to others the active recuperation of history that has been taking place in the Americas.

Usually official history is told by the "victors" and those who hold economic power and control over the mass media. They have no interest in telling the (hi)story of people taking their lives into their own hands, and instead rewrite history in their own interests, emptying it of agency and content, changing the past to influence the present, with the goal of conditioning the future. The struggle around words, concepts and language is crucial, since there are practices linked to them.

Our history, the history from below, is one we have to tell, with our own stories, our own language and our our conceptual frameworks. In this book we introduce a few concepts that come from concrete experiences and practices in a number of movements in Latin America. These are a very small selection of the many ways people around the world are retaking their lives through self organization and the creation of new ways of being.

Among the concepts we explore are Territory, Assembly, Rupture, Popular Power, Horizontalism, *Autogestión* (self-administration), and

Protagonism. Examples of each term are drawn from different Latin American communities of struggle, from the spreading of *Horizontalidad* with the popular rebellion in Argentina, and the concept of Territory seen in Bolivia and Mexico, to the construction of Popular Power in the *Consejos Comunales* in Venezuela, and the vision of interconnected human diversity articulated in the call for "one world in which many worlds fit" by the indigenous Zapatista communities in Chiapas, Mexico.

Now, on to what the new movements are doing, and their secret rendezvous with history.

Colectivo Cordyceps, Mexico City

THE WALK OF THE NEW

In Cairo, Egypt, the people who gathered in Tahrir Square declared *Kefaya!* (Enough!).

In Syntagma Square in Athens, Greece, the people hung banners declaring, in Spanish, *¡Ya Basta!* (Enough is enough!).

In Spain, the people call out for *¡Democracia Real Ya!* (Real democracy now!).

In the United States and throughout the world, people occupy spaces, participate in assemblies and take to the streets saying, *We are the 99%!*

NEW SOCIAL RELATIONSHIPS AND A NEW COMMON LANGUAGE

We are living in a time of uprisings, movements and moments against economic crises and the politics of representation. *Kefaya!*, *¡Ya Basta!* and *Enough!* are shouted by millions against an untenable situation—and resonate with the powerful affirmations *Democracia Real Ya!* and *We are the 99%!* The use of the exclamation point reflects passion and determination. These are shouts of anger, manifestations of collective power and the strength of people's voices in the songs of joy in finding one another.

There have been numerous historic epochs in which something massive and "new" sweeps the globe: the revolutions and revolts of the mid 1800s; the powerful working-class struggles of the early 1900s; the tremendous political and cultural shifts and anti-colonial struggles of the 1960s, to name only three. We believe we have entered another significant historic epoch. This one is marked by an ever-increasing global rejection of representative democracy and, simultaneously, a massive coming together of people who were not previously organized, using direct democratic forms to begin to reinvent ways of being together. Through use of the

Internet, Twitter and Facebook many of today's movements are connected in ways not possible in the past. These new technological forms have helped in spreading information, mobilizing and communicating. But this should not be confused with a "social network revolution," a description many in the media have used. The communication tools helped, but the essence and what's "new" in today's movements is the collective construction of new social relationships—creating new spaces and territories.

Also new, with the direct democratic forms, are similar global ways of speaking about this new social creation. The word horizontal, for example, is used in English, Spanish, Arabic and Greek to describe aspects of these new relationships. People organize in assemblies—calling them "assemblies" and "gatherings" rather than terms such as "meetings"—use similar forms in these assemblies, and share the experience of doing so in public space, often taking it over and occupying it, even if for only a period of time. Within occupied spaces, people then organize internal forms of conflict resolution, from the mediation group in Occupy Wall Street to the "security" teams in Egypt and Greece, and a group with a very similar intention called "Respect" in Spain. If you were to compare scenes from Tahrir Square in Cairo, Syntagma Square in Athens, Zuccotti Park in New York, and Puerta del Sol in Madrid, to name only a few of the thousands, you would see very similar occupations, with elements including free libraries, child care and health services, food, legal support, media and art. The forms of organization and relationships created in the spaces, all using direct democracy, are unique to the needs of each occupation, but at the same time so much alike that they constitute a new global phenomenon.

Also similar globally is a process of reterritorialization of the movements after a few months. Since the intention of the movements is to transform not only an occupied plaza or square but society as a whole, the plaza is more of a starting point, and over time people begin to move more and more into spheres that relate more directly to beginning to retake and control their own lives. Thus, around the world there has been a shift into neighborhoods and workplaces, to focus on local needs yet at the same time come together to coordinate.

For example, in Athens there are now several dozen neighborhood assemblies that meet together every Sunday to have an assembly of assemblies. These gatherings serve to coordinate citywide, including against newly imposed taxes and costs to health care. In Spain we see the same process of reterritorialization in nationally organized eviction prevention that is based in neighborhoods and then networked regionally. In the United States there is also an increase in neighborhood-based organizing as well as neighborhood and citywide eviction prevention and foreclosure defense. People continue to use the plazas and squares as places to gather, have assemblies and sometimes occupy, but the form of territorial construction is shifting, and again, this is being done in a way that is consistent globally.

RECUPERATING LANGUAGE AND VOICE

Many words and phrases have come into common global usage through similar processes of rejection and creation. While many of the words and phrases used in the current global movements are new for movements, or at least new in their current usages, they are often, if not always, laden with context and history. And in this case, the history of the "new" language also emerged from movements seeking to describe what they were creating and doing in ways not previously used—also in many cases drawing on words and phrases with histories, but ones that then, as now, have taken on new meanings based on the new context. The retaking and rediscovering of words and language is a part of the same process of the people finding their own voices with the new usages of direct democracy. As people recuperate their voices—voices they did not have under representational forms of democracy— they find themselves as well. The movements recognize this new agency and protagonism and name it—because naming things is a powerful process in the retaking of history and life. The claim for voice and language is a claim for real democracy.

RUPTURE

The emergence of the new movements is seen by many as a rupture, a breaking with a past way of doing things, as reflected in the widespread use of versions of *¡Ya Basta!, Kefaya!* and even the language of *ruptura*/rupture itself. It is a break with past forms of organization and social relationships, and in the break lies the creation of new ways of being and organizing. This break creates new landscapes that reflect a shift in power relationships, witnessed in multiple ways: from new ways of seeing and being from within movements and society at large, to different dynamics with regard to institutional power. While this is new, it is also true that there is a long history in many parts of the world where this same framework was and is used to describe this experience, from the Zapatistas emerging onto the world scene in 1994 declaring *¡Ya Basta!* to five hundred years of colonialism and domination, to the popular rebellion in Argentina singing on December 19 and 20, 2001, *¡Que Se Vayan Todos!* (They all must go!).

DEMOCRACY AND HORIZONTALISM

One of the most significant things we believe the new movements around the globe have accomplished is making democracy a question. They are challenging and refusing the privileging of economic interests over political and social ones. They even challenge the separation of the economic, the political and the social into different and autonomous spheres. This also implies a challenging of politicians' rule over society, and assumes that the people can govern themselves. Most of the new movements over the past year are practicing forms of direct democracy, and are doing so in public spaces, from Tahrir Square in Egypt to the plazas and parks of Spain, Greece, Europe and the United States. Consistent with the similar forms of organization is a similar language to articulate these new forms. What the movements declare is "Democracy First!" This is not how the political system under which we live functions. Under neoliberal capitalism, those with economic power make decisions related to issues of property and the economy, and then political decisions follow to support the economic decisions that have already been made.

The Occupy movements turn this on its head and say, "No!" First comes democracy, first people decide, and this political reality is inseparable from economic and social issues. This re-linking of political, social and economic relationships is at the heart of the Occupy movements. The embrace of direct and participatory democracy is one of the most visible "new" things in the global movements, but one that is grounded in a long global history, from many of the movements in the 1960s and early '70s to the Zapatistas in Chiapas Mexico, beginning in 1994; from the widespread use of *horizontalidad* in Argentina as of 2001 to the rupture created by the popular uprising in Venezuela in 1989, the *Caracazo*, in which autonomous popular movements in the 1990s expressed their will in the slogan "We don't want to be government, we want to govern." And going back further to different Councilist movements in the first half of the twentieth century—from the Council Communists in Europe, the Anarchists and POUM (Workers' Party of Marxist Unification) in the Spanish Revolution and the anarcho-syndicalists in Latin America and Europe—the aim and practice was direct and participatory democracy, in various forms.

RECUPERATION

The new movements do not first look to others, or expect others to solve their problems, but together are finding ways to take back—recuperate—what they consider to be a right. In the United States and Spain, one way this is being done is through foreclosure defense: the disruption of auction proceedings and the occupying of peoples' homes to prevent the eviction order from being carried out. In Greece some neighborhood assemblies are organizing the blocking of cash registers in hospitals, so that people do not have to pay the newly imposed cost of health care. Sometimes the result of this is that laws are changed or rules modified, as has been the case in a few municipalities in Spain where the local governments have ordered the police not to carry out evictions, or as with a few neighborhoods in Athens where the local governments have put a hold on the collection of new taxes in response to neighborhood assemblies' refusing to pay, en masse. Instead of setting up demands and expecting institutional power to react, people are constructing power together, popular power.

Recuperation is a manifestation of this "new" way the movements are looking at power and autonomy—taking back what is ours. And while it is new now, it is also a form that has been used by the Landless Movement (MST) in Brazil, beginning in the 1980s, taking over land upon which to create new societies, with schools, clinics and the growing of crops; and by the workers in Argentina, coming together as a movement in 2001 and *recuperando* (recuperating) their workplaces, using the slogan of the MST (Occupy, Resist, Produce) and putting their workplaces back to work, with horizontal forms of workers control.

TERRITORIO

The new horizontal social relationships being created are generally forming in geographic space, from neighborhood assemblies in Greece and Spain meeting on street corners, to the constant attempts of Occupy to gather and take over public spaces such as parks. While there is a long tradition of gathering in public spaces in Europe, the current use of public space as a base for the new political social relationships and construction is relatively "new" in these countries. This experience, however, goes back decades in Latin America, when people who (increasingly) were not based in workplaces organized mass protests, and often did so by occupying major road arteries. As they occupied and shut something down, they simultaneously opened something else up—organizing horizontal assemblies and creating prefigurative survival structures for necessities such as food, medicine, child support and trainings. This form of organization took place (and continues to) in regions throughout Ecuador; with the struggles of the Unemployed Workers Movements in Argentina; with the MST in Brazil; and in El Alto Bolivia, among other cities and towns, and in small forms in the thousands of indigenous landless settlements among the Aymara, Quechua, Mapuche, Ayamara and many other native communities. Often these new spaces of autonomous construction are called *territorios* (territories)— speaking to the new landscape that is both physical but also conceptual.

One of the many beautiful things in the new movements is the multiplicity of paths created and desired. There is not one static or pre-stated goal, but instead a process of walking toward desires, and doing so prefiguratively, manifesting the desired future in day-to-day relationships. This is not to be confused with seeing only the process and momentary social relationships as the goal—not at all—rather, we see that as the movement develops, as assemblies take place, people involved in the process change, and as individuals change, the group and territories of construction change—the movement changes, then again individuals are changed. This dynamic of change has an effect/affect on the politics and choices that assemblies and movements make. An ultimate goal and strategy are not predefined but are worked toward, constantly, necessarily changing as we move together, walking, asking questions. Previous movements in Latin America in the 1960s, especially those connected to Liberation Theology, used the framework of *"Hacer el Camino al Andar"* (Making the Road by Walking). The Zapatista communities speak of this similar process as *"Caminar Preguntando"* (To Walk Asking Questions). These examples reflect the multiple histories that help create multiple open-ended paths.

THE SECRET RENDEZVOUS WITH HISTORY AND THE PRESENT

Walter Benjamin wrote of memory and history as a "secret rendezvous between past generations and our own."[1] The secret is not something that is known and not told, but something a great deal more subtle and ambiguous. When we speak of things being "new" in the movements, it is a reflection of their newness in terms of our lived experiences. And when we write various histories to these experiences, which we argue are often very similar, the similarities are frequently so remarkable that it seems as if one is just taken directly from the other. This phenomenon does not take away from newness, the opposite really. Today's movements are finding or creating places where the new meets the old, offering spaces of *encuentro*—encounter and meeting— where new and emerging social relationships creatively mix with many hundreds if not thousands of years of collective experimenting with the various forms of relating, rebellion and struggle.

We offer this meeting place so we may best learn from one another, and especially so we may learn from our various positive experiences as well as the negative ones. It is not

---

1   Walter Benjamin, "Geschichtsphilosophische Thesen," in *Zur Kritik der Gewalt und andere Aufsätze*, Walter Benjamin (Frankfurt a. M.: Suhrkamp, 1965), p. 88.

about fearing a repetition of history, since history does not repeat, but about seeing more clearly some of the many places the movements have come from, so we can walk along further together, from different parts of the world and from our many generations. *Caminar preguntando.*

Our book offers only the slightest of glances, and only into the past twenty years of creation and resistance in Latin America. This could be a multivolume project—especially considering that radical and revolutionary history is not often available to us, particularly the more autonomous movements and understandings of our collective history.

So let us retake our history and bring it along in our present, so as to learn more and find more places of *encuentro* and rendezvous that can be less secret.

Imnop, Brooklyn

·RUPTURE

OPENLY DEFINED: A break, actual or in the imaginary, with previous ways of being, seeing and relating change, in this case opening the way for more emancipatory relationships with greater solidarity. Ruptures can range from economic crisis and "natural" disasters to strikes, mass civil disobedience, rebellions and uprisings.

Families sat at home, many before their television sets, in an evening that began the way so many others had: what to watch, what to make for dinner, the regular nightly questions. Then a TV newscaster appeared on every channel and announced that from that moment on, all bank accounts were frozen. Silence in the house. The economic crisis had fully arrived. People sat in silence, staring at the TV. They waited, they watched and they waited. And then it was heard, outside one window and then another, outside one balcony and another, neighborhood by neighborhood: . . . tac!, tac tac!, tac tac tac! . . . Families went to their windows , went out onto their balconies, and saw what was making the sound. The sound was people banging spoons on pans, spatulas on pots, the sound of the cacerolazo². The sound became a wave, and the wave began to flood the streets. We heard it, and then

---

2   *Cacerola* literally means kitchen pan, and the *cacerolazo* is the collective banging of pots and pans. This tactic has now spread to the student struggle in Quebec, as well as to New York and other cities around the world.

on the television sets accompanying our solitude, we saw it; newscasters, dumbfounded, captured the first cacerolaceros, people in slippers, shorts, robes and tank tops, with children on their shoulders, entire families, out in the streets, tac!, tac tac!, tac tac tac!, hitting their pots and pans. What they were saying was not expressed in words—it was done, bodies spoke, and spoke by the thousands and hundreds of thousands. Tac!, tac tac!, in slippers tac tac!, old people, tac tac!, children, tac tac tac!, the cacerolazo had begun.

The institutions of power did not know what to do, they declared a state of emergency in the morning, falling back on what had always been done. Law and Order. But the people broke with the past, with what had been done, and no longer stayed at home in fear, they came into the streets with even more bodies and sounds. And then the sounds, the tac tac tac!, turned into a song. It was a shout of rejection, and a song of affirmation. ¡Que se vayan todos! (They all must go!) was sung, and sung together with one's neighbor. It was not just a shout against what was, but it was a song sung together, by the thousands and hundreds of thousands. People sang and banged pots and greeted one another, kissing the cheeks of neighbors, really seeing one another for the first time. It was a rupture with the past. It was a rupture with obedience, and a rupture with not being together, with not knowing one another. It was a rupture that cracked open history, upon which vast new histories were created.

Rupture is a break that can come from many places, always shifting both the ways people organize, including power relationships, as well as the ways people see things. Sometimes the detonator is something that happens and produces unexpected or seemingly surprisingly consequences, as in Argentina or the *Caracazo* in Venezuela, and sometimes movements facilitate the rupture, as with the Zapatistas in Chiapas or the Occupy movements.

Rupture can be a break that occurs because of external circumstances, things like earthquakes, floods, fires or economic collapse. These ruptures often inspire thousands, even hundreds of thousands, to come together and help one another. When massive collapse happens, often those formal institutions of power also collapse, or go into crisis. People then look to one another, begin to try and find solutions together, and often do so in ways that are more "effective" and definitely more empowering, "affective," than had it been done elsewhere or by others.

In the current movements, arising in 2010 and 2011, rupture came upon us, seemingly surprisingly, though in many places around the world there was some organization in advance. This includes the New York City General Assembly organizing throughout the summer in response to the *Adbusters* call, and *¡Democracia real ya!* in Spain meeting and gathering others for the first assemblies, before the occupation of Puerta del Sol—yet not imagining that there would be such a lasting and massive occupation. Rupture can be when many things break open—our imaginations, societies' imagination, the idea of the possible and impossible—and this can shift the public dialogue about what is and what is possible. Central to the idea of rupture is that ways of seeing things fundamentally change, and in response people start to organize and relate with one another differently. To speak with movement participants around the globe now, in 2012, many use the same language to describe what took place with the Plaza and Park occupations, the same word even, translated everywhere as rupture. From *ruptura* in Spanish (literally rupture) to *kefaya* (enough) in Arabic.

Throughout Latin America the language of rupture is used to describe the decisive moments when things break open—freeing new relationships, creating new landscapes and shifting relationships of power. In Bolivia the "Cochabamba Water War" was a clear rupture. Protests in the Bolivian city of Cochabamba broke out after the government privatized the water and gave the concessions to a U.S. transnational company, Bechtel. Bechtel raised prices immediately, so that people had to pay water bills that were up to 35 percent of their monthly income. Bechtel also forbade the traditional irrigation systems of peasants, prohibiting the collection of rainwater, considering it their property, essentially privatizing rainwater. The people of Cochabamba and the surrounding peasant communities began organizing in response in 1999. Between January and April of 2000, many thousands of people organized in the streets, resisting both the police and the military, with the result that the city streets were effectively controlled by the protesters. Finally government authorities did not dare to show themselves on the streets of Cochabamba, and the police and military retreated to their camps and bases. The central government was forced to turn back the decision to privatize water. It was a massive victory for the people, and a rupture in the relationship of power between the "people organized" and the government and its forces of repression.

For the people of Venezuela, the rupture that has led to the current process of struggle and creation began on February 27, 1989, with the explosion of *El Caracazo*. The rebellion was caused by a situation of dramatically increasing poverty. Annual inflation had reached 100 percent. There were shortages and speculation with regard to food and most basic necessities. More than half the population was hungry. These abysmal conditions had resulted from a program of austerity and structural adjustment implemented by President Carlos Andrés Pérez, following International Monetary Fund (IMF) guidelines, that enabled changes in labor laws, more leeway in the hiring and firing of workers, and the privatization of state-owned services and enterprises, such as the telephone company. The final detonator was when on the morning of February 27, people went to ride their neighborhood bus and found that the fares had doubled overnight. Public rage was immediate. Throughout Caracas people responded by destroying buses, and then setting them alight. From there, people began to walk down the hills from the poor neighborhoods, taking what they needed and wanted—looting. The rebellion spread to all Venezuelan cities, involving more than one million people. In response, the government ordered the police and the army to suppress the uprising, killing thousands. It is said, even if not officially confirmed, that the government had left the country and come back after the uprising was suppressed.

The Caracazo was a rupture. People suddenly realized their potential collective power, and that with it they could even chase out a government. But it also showed that if they could not build their own structures of self-administration, old forms of institutional power could again return.

The middle ranks of the army were the ones ordered to carry out the massacre. The outcome enforced the conviction among the already secretly organized leftist "Bolivarians"[3]

---

3   Revolutionary and emancipatory Bolivarianism is inspired by Simón Bolívar (1783–1830), Venezuelan by birth, who led Colombia, Venezuela, Ecuador, and Bolivia to independence, and set the foundations for democratic thought; by his teacher, the philosopher Simón Rodríguez (1769–1854), who frequented utopian socialist circles in France in the early 19th century; by the peasant general of the federal war, Ezequiel Zamora (1817–1860); and by the indigenous and Afro-Venezuelan resistance. Bolivarianism is not so much an ideology as it is a set of values orienting a process of seeking. It came up in the revolutionary left, which proclaimed a civil-military uprising as the Venezuelan path to revolution, and various currents began to infiltrate

in the armed forces that it was necessary to act quickly to stop the regime. And the experience of having been ordered to shoot their own people convinced thousands of soldiers to join the different secret leftist and revolutionary groups inside the army, particularly the group led by Hugo Chávez and other young officers.

In February and November of 1992, there were two civil-military uprisings. The military coordinated its uprisings with leftist groups and organizations from poor neighborhoods, and even some armed revolutionary militias and former guerrilla fighters. The civil-military uprisings failed, and hundreds of soldiers were killed by loyal troops. Hundreds more were imprisoned. But knowing that at least a portion of army members were with the people and ready even to risk their lives on a path of no return such as an armed uprising, gave the people hope and strength.

A fundamental change in Venezuela was a widespread feeling that revolutionary change no longer seemed out of reach. This meant another important rupture. Together with the *Caracazo*, the civil-military uprisings were constitutive of the Bolivarian process. In the midst of the crisis of the established powers, popular movements adopted more and more autonomous positions, moving from specific demands

---

the army or to clandestinely recruit military personnel. This led to a clandestine military organization with the goal of overthrowing the government and building a more just system. Chávez was among the founding members of the biggest organization in the army.

around concrete problems to demands for self-determination, self-management, and constituent power.

HORIZONTALIDAD, HORIZONTALISM, HORIZONTAL

OPENLY DEFINED: *Horizontalidad* is a form of social relations established and sustained through non-hierarchical forms of communication. *Horizontalidad* implies the use of direct democracy and the striving for consensus— inclusive processes in which attempts are made to ensure that everyone is heard and new relationships are created.

A fire is burning at the intersection of Corrientes and Federico Lacroze in the city of Buenos Aires. More than one hundred people of all ages are gathered around, some still dressed from work, in high heels, skirts and jackets; others come from home, in housecoats, T-shirts and flip-flops. They are high school students and teenagers, middle-aged workers, children and the very elderly. They are men and women. They gather and form a circle around a fire blazing in the intersection.

The noises of the city are all around. Yet there is a quiet.

There is a quiet that can be felt, a quiet that is respect, a quiet that is a growing dignity, the quiet of listening. An older woman is speaking of how to organize the upcoming weeks' free medical ser-

vice, which will be offered by a doctor from another neighborhood assembly.

The questions of where the medical service will take place, and how to get the needed supplies are on the table for discussion. It is a question of the health of the children in the neighborhood. The topic is serious. The listening is serious. The quiet is serious.

People take turns speaking. Some talk over others, and the facilitator is often ignored. Yet all manage to speak and to be heard. It is the quiet insurgent noise of horizontalidad. The group finally reaches a consensus, and the quiet changes, a song emerges, the joyous song sung on the days that the popular rebellion began. "Ohhh, que se vayan todos, que no quede ni uno solo . . . ohhh . . ." This is horizontalidad in Argentina.

To participate in any of the assemblies taking place throughout the world generally means to stand or sit in a circle, with a handful of facilitators, and speak and listen in turn, with general guidelines and principles of unity, and then together work to discuss and reach consensus, a general agreement on whatever issue is raised. If one were to ask a participant about this process, they most likely would explain the need to listen to one another, feeling that in society they are excluded from meaningful participation, and perhaps they might use the language of direct or participatory democracy. Often in these conversations, some version of the horizontal will arise, whether in the description or desired goal.

Horizontalidad, horizontality and horizontalism are words that encapsulate the ideas upon which many of the social relationships in the new global movements are grounded. *Horizontalidad* is a new way of articulating this relationship, based in affective and trust-based politics. It is a dynamic social relationship. It is not an ideology or political program that must be met so as to create a new society. Horizontal relationships are a break with the logic of representation and vertical ways of organizing.

Horizontalidad is a practice used by social movements and groups, but when the conversation moves in the direction of mass assemblies and autonomous governance, there might also be a need for structures that, while using nonrepresentative forms, are not either creating the same sort of social relationships possible with *horizontalidad*. (Spokes councils, the Zapatista form of self-governance, and the Communes in Venezuela are three such examples.)

The word *horizontalidad* was first heard in the days after the popular rebellion in Argentina in December 2001. No one recalls where it came from or who might have said it first. It was a new word, and emerged from a new practice. The practice was people coming together, looking to one another, and without anyone in charge or having power over another, beginning to find ways to solve their problems together. And through doing this together, they were creating a new relationship—both the process of making decisions, and the way they wanted to relate in the future were horizontal. What this meant was, and still is, to be discovered in the practice, or as the Zapatistas say, in the walk, questioning as we walk.

The rebellion in Argentina came in response to a growing economic crisis that had already left hundreds of thousands without work, and many thousands hungry. The state provided no possible way out. In response, first one person, and then another, and then hundreds, thousands and hundreds of thousands came out into the street, banging pots and pans, *cacerolando*. They were not led by any party, and were not following any slogans, they merely sang, "*¡Que se vayan todos! ¡Que no quede ni uno solo!*" (They all must go! Not even one should remain!). Within two weeks, four national governments had resigned.

One of the most significant things about the social movements that have emerged in Argentina since the 2001 popular rebellion, is how generalized the experience of *horizontalidad* was and has remained, among the middle class organized into neighborhood assemblies; the unemployed organizing in neighborhoods; and workers taking over—recuperating their workplaces. *Horizontalidad*, with a rejection of hierarchy and political parties, became the norm. And now, in 2012, the assumption that people often begin with as they continue to organize is that any new movement effort or struggle will be horizontal. This can be seen today in the hundreds of assemblies up and down the Andes fighting against international mining companies, and the thousands of *bachilleratos*—alternative high school diploma programs organized by former assembly participants, housed in recuperated workplaces.

Horizontalidad is a living word, reflecting an ever-changing experience. While months after the popular rebellion many movement participants spoke of their relationships as horizontal to describe the new forms of decision-making, years after the rebellion, those continuing to build new movements, spoke of *horizontalidad* as a goal as well as a tool. Social relationships are still deeply affected by capitalism and hierarchy, and thus by the sort of power dynamics they promote in collective and creative spaces, especially how people relate to one another in terms of economic resources, gender, race, access to information and experience. *Horizontalidad* has to be understood as an open-ended social process, an active act of seeking, rather than a final end, since living under capitalism makes total equality of relationships impossible. It would be an illusion to think that a "happy island of horizontalism" can be created in the middle of the sea of capitalism.

Movements around the globe using horizontal forms of assemblies and relationships, from Spain and Greece to London and the United States, are also beginning to reflect more deeply on the challenges, similarly reflecting that *horizontalidad* is not a thing, but a process. One such reflection is a critique of the belief that the naming of a practice alone can conjure the behavior. Similarly, conflating the naming of a practice with a person's identity—"I am horizontal," for example—can confuse the fact that it is only made real in practice, not by the naming. Even worse, there can be the possibility of creating a hierarchy in our very efforts to combat hierarchal structures, for example, by asserting that I am more horizontal than you are, or that our collective has the most horizontal practices.

The idea that *horizontalidad* can be a thing, something that exists by its invocation, is not quite right. This can create more than confusion; sometimes it can lead to anger and frustration. If a person is told that all have an equal voice, that there is no hierarchy, and that relationships are all prefigurative, and then that person has an experience of not feeling heard or respected (or prefigured!), she is likely to feel betrayed. If collectively we do not see *horizontalidad* as a process, we are less likely to do the hard work of breaking down hierarchy and trying to create power with one another. It is important to always make clear and always be aware of the fact that the naming of a practice does not mean it is being actually manifested.

PODER POPULAR—
POPULAR POWER

OPENLY DEFINED: Popular power is the capacity of the marginalized and the oppressed to change power relations through processes of organization, training and coordination in order to govern their own lives. Building popular power means building social relations contrary to the logic of capital.

We are in Sala de Batalla Alicia Benítez, the community center of the "Eje de MACA" Commune Under Construction in the Greater Caracas area. We are in Petare, which is said to be Latin America's largest poor neighborhood (sometimes called barrio, villa, favela or shantytown.) Thirty communities that are organized in Communal Councils have united to create a Commune and all decide from below, in their local assemblies, what to do in their neighborhoods. The barrios, the informal and marginalized neighborhoods, make up about 70 percent of Caracas. Infrastructure in the barrios is precarious; they lack basic services, there is little to no public space, and most of the dwellings are built into the hillside and connected to one another through unevenly built narrow stairs and walkways.

"Look," says Pablo to the government employee offering to build a place to store and sell food at far below market price by eliminating intermediaries and speculation, "one thing has to be clear, we

decided in the community that we will administer this place."[4] Yusmeli, joining the conversation, says, "We also have to be able to sell other food, for example by connecting directly with producers."[5] The government official agrees, he will bring maps to discuss the construction with the community. The Commune already has two Enterprises of Social Communal Property: a passenger transport system with six four-wheel-drive jeeps, and a center for the distribution of liquid gas for cooking. Most of the Communal Councils have small community enterprises such as bakeries, a cobbler and even small agricultural production. To set up the Commune enterprises, first all the Communal Councils held assemblies and discussed what they needed most. Then they held workshops with a facilitator from the Ministry of Communes and discussed the project in detail, including the organizational and decision-making structure for the enterprises. The result was approved by the neighborhood assemblies of the Communal Councils.

The liquid gas distribution center was built by the national petrol company PDVSA and is administered by the community. "It started to work in April 2011 and immediately we could pay four people to work there at a dignified salary, even while the gas cylinder is sold at just 20 percent of the usual market price. As well, those most in need, like unemployed

4   Pablo Arteaga, Comuna de MACA, interview with Dario Azzellini, Caracas, Venezuela, August 8, 2011.
5   Yusmeli Patiño, interview with Dario Azzellini, Caracas, Venezuela, August 8, 2011.

single mothers get it free," explained Lorenzo,[6] who used to be a lawyer for private firms. Lorenzo, together with Pablo and Yusmeli, is one of the driving forces behind the Commune and works in the communal transport enterprise. "We got six vehicles from the Ministry of Transport and we started serving the Commune on the highest parts of the hill, since they had the worst service."

The communities of the Eje de MACA Commune also have brought doctors, dentists and literacy educators to their communities. Most of the initiatives took place with a combination of self-organization and institutional support. The first thing is always self-organization, "and even if the institutions are supposed to support the communities, most of the time you have to fight to get what you want and the way you want it," explains Yusmeli. "But we confront the institutions and refuse to accept what we don't want. We are people's power."

The specific phrase "popular power" is not generally used in the Occupy movements, but the phenomenon of creating popular power is widespread. The ways this is done are so close to the ways that popular power has been articulated in Latin America over the past decades that some historicization and context is useful.

Historically, popular power had been understood as social forces that build parallel struc-

---

6   Lorenzo Martini, interview with Dario Azzellini, Caracas, Venezuela, August 8, 2011.

tures in a revolutionary process, creating a situation of dual power. After consolidation of the new "real" power—the party and/or the revolutionary state—popular power would be subordinated to them. In the new movements, since the 1990s, first in Latin America and then beyond, the construction of popular power has been understood as a path and goal. The construction of parallel structures is not seen as transitional until the "takeover" of the state but as the central element of building a new society, while the old structures still exist. It is not a fully formed concept, but rather a process of seeking and creation, nourished by centuries of experiences, forms of organization, and struggles of subalterns (people who are marginalized, indigenous, formerly enslaved, workers, members of impoverished communities and so on).

The forms that popular power can take differ a great deal. Anything that enables the people to administer aspects of their lives on their own, and whatever gives them the power to make their own decisions and improve their own autonomous process of constructing new social relations, can be seen as part of popular power. While some mechanisms of popular power might simply be directed to carrying out new alternative projects, others are constructing new institutionality. Popular power can be expressed through creating a community soup kitchen, recuperating a workplace, or by forming a network of community-controlled radio stations, it can also been seen with new forms of local self-administration, a local assembly of people debating their own needs or an assembly discussing public initiatives and taking a collective position toward them.

In Oaxaca, Mexico, more then 350 groups and rank-and-file organizations founded the Popular Assembly of the People of Oaxaca (APPO) in June 2006. Teachers had been on strike for over two weeks, occupying the central plaza (*Zócalo*), and then within two days of their brutal eviction, the community came together to form the APPO. The APPO developed a popular council as a tool for popular power. The protesters in Oaxaca forced the police and government authorities out of the city, took over radio stations and various buildings, and defended the city with thousands of barricades. After five months of successful defense and a deepening sophistication of the structures of democracy and alternative infrastructure, the Zócalo was stormed by thousands of special police forces, and with massive repression the Zócalo was cleared in November 2006.[7] The collective experience and practice of indigenous people, land workers, barrio inhabitants, students and workers made it possible to set up popular power and prevent the government

---

7   During the "Commune of Oaxaca" at least twenty-three people were killed by government troops or state-affiliated paramilitary forces. Among those killed was U.S. activist and independent media maker Brad Will.

from intervening in the popular construction for over five months. Some have referred to this period as the Commune of Oaxaca.

In Venezuela, the Communal Councils are the most advanced mechanism of local self-organization and popular power. They are non-representative bodies with directly democratic participation, parallel to the elected representative institutions. In 2005, the Communal Councils began forming from below. In January 2006, President Chávez adopted the initiative and began to help it spread. A law followed in April 2006. The Communal Councils in urban areas encompass some 150 to 400 families; in rural zones, twenty families; and in indigenous regions, ten families. In 2011 there were approximately 40,000 CCs in Venezuela. Their decision-making body is called the Assembly of Neighbors. It decides the geographic territory of the communities and has to approve the projects developed in local Work Commissions. The entire community elects spokespeople for its Work Commission, which is tasked with coordinating collectively made decisions, and is not itself empowered to make decisions.

Given the exceptional situation in Venezuela, with a government partly engaged in supporting forms of popular power, people's groups have a different and stronger relationship with the state than in most other countries. As with autonomy, the question is whether structures of popular power can maintain their own spaces for debate, decisions and construction or whether they become co-opted by the state and loose their own agency and agenda. This is an ongoing tension in the process of construction in Venezuela. The government and its institutions are supportive and an obstacle at the same time. And the relationship between institutions and self-organization is characterized by cooperation and conflict. Institutions tend to consolidate and expand their power, not wanting to give it up, and by institutional logic, the development and growth of parallel powers and structures are seen as a threat to their existence. In Venezuela this contradiction is especially sharp, with large segments of the institutions of power supporting the autonomous development of the movements, yet with other large sectors resisting this development, even creating obstacles and trying to control them.

In today's movements, the construction of popular power is seen in multiple ways and on various levels. It is most advanced in those countries, towns and cities where there has been an ongoing territorial construction, where there are neighborhood assemblies that are working to defend people in the neighborhood as well as creating more of a community. For example, as of May 2012 there were forty-five neighborhood assemblies in Athens, each one focusing on the needs of the local populations—organizing things such as barter networks and direct exchanges with agricultural producers and consumers—as well as on broader issues such as refusal to pay the increase in taxes placed on electric bills. This refusal then became more coordinated citywide, in part through the weekly assembly of assemblies, where all the neighborhoods participate, and as a result a number of municipalities have now declared a "hold" on the increase of the electricity tax. This organizing together in the neighborhoods and across neighborhoods, manifesting what people need, not asking for something to be done, is a demonstration of popular power.

Similarly, other manifestations of popular power can be seen in Spain and the United States, in the foreclosure-defense movements that organize to keep people in their homes, resisting foreclosures and eviction. Even if, in the end, the bank or financial authority makes a compromise with the demands of the struggles, it is the people organized who are together constructing popular power, agreeing on what they need and want, and then democratically making that happen, despite and in direct confrontation and non-compliance with existing laws or regulations.

The occupation and use of public space offers yet another deeply significant expression of popular power. Within a number of weeks, hundreds of thousands of people across the

United States began to take for granted that if an assembly was called many, sometimes hundreds or even thousands, would come together and create it. This does not mean that an occupation of a space that includes an encampment, with tents and so on, could be organized without planning, but the assumption was and is that if an assembly is desired, one just names a public space and it will occur. Before September 17, 2011, this was not an assumption, and in most cities and towns a gathering of more than twenty or thirty people required a permit. This is no longer even an issue. Assemblies take place in parks, in plazas and even on street corners, and no permits have been requested for them since September 17. People together, organized, not filing for permits, but coming together and affirming with one another our power, have created this new space, a space constructed by popular power.

ASSEMBLIES AND *ENCUENTROS*

OPENLY DEFINED: Face-to-face gatherings of people, formed with the desire to share, discuss and sometimes come to common agreement in a directly democratic manner.

It was the night of September 17, 2011. More than 2,000 people filled Zuccotti Park. No one knew what to expect, but many were filled with anticipation. As night fell, the general assembly began. It was intense, inspiring, and went on for hours. As 10:00 p.m. approached, thinking the park might close, proposals became more concrete. A consensus was reached: We would occupy. Thousands of hands went up in silent applause—twinkling— and then we began a chant—no, a song, really, and a song with a call and response. The facili- tators asked: "What does democracy look like?" Thousands responded: "This is what democracy looks like!" People were singing, jumping up and down and dancing, full of joy and a sense of power.

Much farther south, four years prior, in an autonomously controlled community, with a Junta de Buen Gobierno (good government junta) facili- tating the participation of international guests, the first-ever Zapatista Women's Encuentro was held. The indigenous rebel women explained, among other things, the following:

> We are going to speak, we women Zapatistas, with compañeras from Mexico and the world, and you will be able to ask questions about how we organize ourselves, the women Zapatistas, more directly with women. We are going to ask that the compañeros (men Zapatistas) help us with logistical questions. Compa- ñeros from Mexico and the world may also come to hear us, but remain silent, the same as our compañeros.
>
> This Third Encuentro, as it will be espe- cially of the women Zapatistas, will be dedi-

cated to Comandanta Ramona, and will take her name. Thus its name is this: Third Encuentro of the Zapatista Peoples with the Peoples of the World: Comandanta Ramona and the Women Zapatistas.[8]

And that is what it was, a gathering of women from around the world, with hundreds of women Zapatistas presenting and discussing what they had been creating together for fourteen years. The space was open and free, a true gathering and meeting of women from around the globe, talking about what was impossible and is now possible.

An integral part of creating direct democracy and *horizontalidad* is the moments of gathering, the intentional coming together in ways so that all can speak and be heard, and often, so decisions can be made. "Assembly" is the name that is frequently used for this, particularly in the past fifteen years. While conventionally it means only a coming together for a common purpose, the autonomous movements in Latin America and the globalization movements have shifted this meaning to imply a search for a desired common ground together, sometimes using the language of consensus, sometimes not. Direct democracy does not necessarily imply consensus. In fact,

---

8   "Convocatoria al 3ffl Encuentro, por la Compañera Everilda, candidata al CCRI," zeztainternazional, August 8, 2007, accessed June 24, 2012, http://zeztainternazional.ezln.org.mx/?p=18.

using the assembly form does not imply any one particular decision-making process in the movements, only that agreement is sought in a directly democratic manner. What this means is that attempts are made for all voices to be heard, using different tools for speaking and using active listening to be as open and inclusive as possible. This is often done through the use of facilitators who have been trained in whatever democratic form the group has chosen, though sometimes it is more of a collective effort, with the group taking responsibility for facilitation and participation. Other times, a group has a prior agreement for forms of participation, similar to ground rules, such as the establishment of a speaking order that alternates between male- and female-identified people speaking during assemblies. Occupy Wall Street, practices a modified speakers' list (stack), in which the list of speakers changes so that those people more "historically marginalized" get moved up higher on the speakers' list; in many other groups, a person can only speak once until all those who wish to speak have also spoken. There are countless such examples of different groups finding ways to make the assembly the most participatory as makes the most sense in that particular location.

Consensus is a formal, but flexible, process of decision-making that is modified in each location to reflect the needs of the people. Consensus is also a term that can be used by many in the assembly process to mean simply that a synthesis of ideas is sought based on all opinions shared during the gathering. Saying that an assembly seeks consensus does not have to mean that all the various potential rules of consensus are applied. Often assemblies use different forms of voting to reach decisions, and even groups that seek consensus can use forms of voting. For example, many of the neighborhood assemblies in Argentina spoke of the consensus they sought, yet did not use many of the tools of the consensus process, but rather talked through all the issues, disagreements and proposals until there was either an agreement or a vote. As we have said, at the most basic level, assemblies are face-to-face gatherings of people, formed with the desire to come to common agreement together in a directly democratic manner.

Important to note here is that the assembly form has emerged throughout history and around the world, especially in times of crisis or rupture. People come together, look to each other, discuss the situation they are in, and often make decisions about what to do. These times of crisis or rupture can range from citywide blackouts, earthquakes and other natural disasters to economic crisis.

Encuentro is a word originating in Latin America and in Spanish, and it is now used around the world, often keeping the word in Spanish. Encuentro also means a coming together, generally with horizontal relational forms, but unlike an assembly, an encuentro does not need to have the desired end of a decision or consensus; it is the gathering, the process, that is the end. The reason for the encuentro is the coming together. The use of encuentro became particularly widespread following the Zapatistas' First Intergalactic Encuentro for Humanity and Against Neoliberalism in 1996. During this encuentro, thousands of people met in liberated Zapatista territory to share experiences and learn what the Zapatistas were doing, as well as to strengthen international solidarity with the autonomous communities.

The Zapatista concept of *"Un Mundo Donde Quepan Muchos Mundos"* (One World in Which Many Worlds Fit) has also been brought into the meaning of encuentro, so that rather than being thought of as a place to make a single unifying program, a gathering is instead a place where all can come together with all of our differences and in diversity.

In some Latin American countries, especially in Venezuela but also in Colombia, Bolivia, Argentina, Guatemala and Peru, the term *"encuentro de saberes"* (encuentro of knowledge) is widely used for gatherings to exchange experience and knowledge without creating a hierarchy from the different forms of knowledge. For example, in an *encuentro de saberes ancestrales indígenas y campesinos de agroecología* (ancestral indigenous and peasants' knowledge of organic farming) indigenous people and peasants, as well as agronomists and ecologists, might take part and share their knowledge. In an *encuentro de saberes pedagógicos* (pedagogical knowledge) teachers, academics and employees of institutions in the field of education might discuss and share their knowledge along with parents, students and activists engaged in popular education.

RECUPERATE

OPENLY DEFINED: The term recuperate, in an emancipatory context, refers to the re-appropriation of something concrete, conceptual or historical, by the people. This is anything from a factory to historical memory. The prefix "re" indicates that it is understood as having belonged to the people before.

Located on Avenue Callao, at the corner of Corrientes, in the center of Buenos Aires, the Hotel Bauen could not be more centrally located. It is a five-minute walk to the Congressional building, across from which is the school and bookstore for the Madres de la Plaza de Mayo. Corrientes is one of the main avenues in Buenos Aires, known for all its shops and restaurants, and this section of Corrientes is also home to many bookstores, theaters and art centers. It is a perfect central place for an occupation, and even better for a recuperation.

When the workers of Hotel Bauen took the plywood off the lobby window and entered the hotel, the intention was to have the entire hotel up and running within the year. Previously a four-star hotel, the Hotel Bauen has more than two hundred rooms, two pools, a massive bronze-filled lobby that includes a grand piano, a full theater, two restaurants, two cafés, two bars, a small print shop and countless offices and other facilities. After months of downsizing the staff, the owners laid off the remaining workers and shut the doors to the hotel in late December 2001. Almost immediately thereafter, a few of the unemployed workers met with workers from some of the other recuperated workplaces and the National Movement for Recuperated Workplaces (MNER) network. Together they made the decision to take over their workplace and run it in common. They began meeting more regularly, and gathered a few dozen of the previous workers to join in the process. In March 2003 they took back their workplace, together with hundreds of supporters from other workplaces, recuperated and not, as well as neighborhood assemblies and the community at large. There are now more than 150 workers running the Hotel Bauen.

The night of the takeover was one filled with tension and fear, but at the same time incredibly joyful. People were ready to fight and resist, but they were simultaneously giddy. Many dozens of workers and neighbors stood and sat around, many chain-smoking, waiting to see if the scouts had any news of police movement. Nothing,

nothing, nothing. Hours passed. At one point, a man sat at the piano and played a song. It was an unforgettable moment, the sort of event that can create chills even now, thinking back on it. Years later, on another trip to Argentina and the Hotel Bauen, there in the hotel music room we found the very same man who had played the piano for all of us in the occupied lobby. He had changed a bit physically, his hair whiter—the results, he jokes, of "all the struggle in fighting for the hotel." But his energy and passion were the same. That night, as we all sat waiting in the lobby, with no electricity except for the few lanterns people had brought with them, Guillermo sat at the piano and began to play a tune, which at that point was little known. A song he had written. A song that now is known throughout the country.

The song:

> *We are the present and the future*
> *To resist and occupy,*
> *The factory will not be closed*
> *We are going to raise it together*
> *The factory will not be closed*
> *We are going to raise it together.*

> *[chorus]*

> *To resist and resist and occupy*
> *To resist and resist and produce.*

The song continues, and over the years it has

been sung with various names of workplaces that are in the process of being recuperated.

The movements of 2011 have been all about occupying and using public space—taking it over, though in the words of movement participants what they are doing is taking it back—seeing it as public space that should be used by the public, thus, recuperating it. In the spaces the movements immediately set up prefigurative structures, structures that support those coming into the plaza with necessities from food, medical and legal aid, to education, libraries, yoga, music, dance, mediation for conflict resolution and even sometimes therapy. The idea is not just to take over a space, but to do something with it that makes it useful and supportive to everyone, productive if you will, just not in the market-value sense of the word. The other key piece of the taking and using of space is that the movements are not doing it as a strategic holding, an occupation with a demand, such that when the demand is met then the occupation ends, as with traditional factory, school or even political office occupations. The new movements' occupations are not pointed upward at institutional power, but across at one another, immediately creating alternatives and a new form of value production. This is recuperation.

Over the past decade the slogan "Occupy, Resist, Produce," beginning with the MST in the 1980s in Brazil and now throughout Latin America with recuperated workplaces, has come to represent one of the seemingly most complicated yet actually most straightforward movements in Latin America today. In Argentina, with more than three hundred Worker-Recuperated Workplaces (*Empresas Recuperadas por sus Trabajadores*), workers are at the forefront of forming new relationships of social change and production, often challenging the capitalist mode of value production.[9]

The process of workplace recuperations in Argentina arose from economic necessity and a total lack of response from bosses, management, owners and the state. As with so many other things related to the popular rebellion of 2001, and the spirit of "*¡Que se vayan todos!*" (They all must go!), workers took the situation into their own hands.

It is also important to note that the recuperations have been taking place not only in traditional factories, such as metal, ceramics and print shops, but in many other sorts of workplaces, such as grocery stores, medical clinics, daily newspapers, schools, bakeries and hotels. In these movements, work is defined by one's

---

9   This refers to the creation of a new sort of value production, one sometimes outside the system of capitalist domination, breaking from the profit motive, alienation and capitalist relationships in the day-to-day relationships to production. It does not mean that the new relationships are beyond capital, but that the relationship to production specifically is changing and is not based on capitalist value, i.e., profit and money alone.

relationship not only to a machine, but to production in general, and in the rethinking of the relationship to production so as to prioritize the needs of workers, their families, the community and the environment.

The process of worker recuperations can be found throughout Latin America with dozens in Brazil, Uruguay and Venezuela, and a few in Colombia and Mexico. The organizational structure they adopt differs from processes of worker control, using everything from directly democratic assemblies to ones that resemble more traditional cooperatives with less direct participation in day-to-day decisions.

Recuperation has been used more broadly than it sense with regard to workplaces or geographic spaces, as with the current Occupy movements. In Mexico and Venezuela, for example, movements speak of the recuperation of memory, history, knowledge and dignity.

Before the March of *1,111 unarmed Zapatistas* to Mexico City in 1997, Subcomandante Marcos declared on behalf of the Indigenous Revolutionary Clandestine Committee General Command of the Zapatista Army of National Liberation: "We are going to recuperate national history for the ones from below. Today it is hijacked by the ones governing, to be killed and buried under the economic indices. We will shout out: Never again a Mexico without us!"[10]

10 Communiqué, August 8, 1997.

An important element in building emancipatory paths is, as Walter Benjamin emphasizes, historical consciousness of the role of past generations. But it is not about "recuperating" an idealized past, nor is it a matter of nostalgia or folklore. In each case, the recuperation requires an adaptation to the present. It is more a "secret rendezvous between past generations and our own."[11] And it is the recuperation of one's own place in history. History is the history of class struggle, said Marx. But the histories of liberation and emancipatory struggles are rarely told. And the ones that have built all we can see, the countless past generations who have given everything for a better world, are rarely mentioned. Recuperating memory and history is mainly a collective process. The past common history and experience is reconstructed to enrich the present and build a common future. In many places in Latin America, especially poor urban areas, the recuperation of the history of one's own neighborhood is often the starting point to build community and collective consciousness.

PROTAGONISM AND SOCIAL PROTAGONISM

OPENLY DEFINED: Protagonism is self-activity and action, as opposed to concepts of delega-

---

11   Benjamin, "Geschichtsphilosophische Thesen," p. 88.

tion and representation. Social protagonism is individual activity, together with others similarly mobilized, interrelated and interdependent in emancipatory action and vision.

"I think the best lesson we, and especially the young people, have learned from the Water War in Cochabamba is that it is possible to change things without having to follow anyone, without depending on the political parties, without needing political parties to mediate. During eight days, every sign and even symbol of the state disappeared in Cochabamba. The army was barracked and the police asked the people for permission to leave the police station. There was no political party, there was not any leader telling anyone what to do. Nobody was telling people what they should do or had to do. That is where people really began to feel that they were the real protagonist in this collective action, one based on a collective horizon, but also built together, in common . . . and that we were doing everything among equals."[12]

The idea of protagonism—the way it has been used by movements over the past two decades—is strongly related to social agency and therefore to direct democracy and participation. For example, in Venezuela, protagonism became more prominent over the course of the 1990s

12 Oscar Olivera, from the Coordinadora del Agua, interview with Marina Sitrin, Cochabamaba, Bolivia, 2007

when movements stopped asking political parties and institutions to solve the problems they faced and began struggling for direct participation and control in their neighborhoods. To distinguish the democratic form of society and governance from the definition and goal used also by liberal and representative democracy, the term "participation" was used in the constitution. This constitution was the product of active participation among grassroots organizations, through working groups (*mesas*), facilitating discussions, which resulted in the document in 1999 in which Venezuela was defined a "participatory and protagonistic democracy."

People in the movements and neighborhood organizations speak regularly about the difference in their participation now, feeling that they were previously not involved in, or allowed access to, the processes and politics that affect their lives. They now call themselves protagonists because they fought and won their political agency, but this also means that people have to organize in order to make things happen. The identification as protagonists, in a massive way, especially among those without any previous organizing experience, happened during the first years of the Chávez government, through government social programs called Missions, in which self-organization of the population was a central element. One example was the literacy campaign "*Yo Sí Puedo*," organized with support from Cubans, who helped to train volunteer facilitators. The literacy process took place in communities where people who desired basic literacy education organized to make it happen. Within the first two years, one and a half million people achieved literacy. Overcoming marginalization through their own protagonism led people to self-organize around other questions concerning their own lives and communities.

Over the course of two years, the culture of participation took hold deeply in the communities, and even people no one expected to participate are now participating in common activities, all for the sake of the common good of the community. Participation is understood as democratization and equal rights:

> Participatory and protagonistic democracy means that we all participate, it is something horizontal, nobody has a rank or anything like that. And it's protagonistic because we are the ones setting the tone. . . . We all participate voluntarily, not because somebody is leading us, we don't have bosses.[13]

In Argentina, the terms protagonism and social protagonism took root after the popular rebellion of 2001. They refer to the newfound agency people felt in acting together to reject

13   Wilson Moya, from the CC Emiliano Hernández, interview with Dario Azzellini, Caracas, Venezuela, January 9, 2007.

long-established patterns of representational politics. This protagonism is found in the more autonomous of the social movements as well as some of the more self-organized communities.

Cándido, a worker from a recuperated print shop in Buenos Aires, once clarified in a conversation that he is not "political," but rather a "protagonist." Many in the autonomous movements in Argentina do not call themselves activists, but rather "protagonists." It is an understanding expressed through terms based on the experience of different relationships, rather than an overarching theory. Through this collective protagonism also arises the need for new ways of speaking of the *"nosotros"* ("we/us") and *"nuestro"* ("our"), as they relate to the *"yo"* ("I").

When workers in the recuperated workplace movements in Argentina and Venezuela refer to the workplaces as "theirs," they do not mean this in a sense of private property, but in a broader collective sense. The workers of Zanón in Argentina (now FaSinPat—*Fábrica Sin Patrón*: Factory Without a Boss) say, *"Zanón Es del Pueblo"* (Zanon is of the people), meaning it is the community mobilized that makes Zanón exist, and that it exists for the people.

Protagonism and social protagonism can sound a lot like just being political, but many who are using this other way of referring to themselves are taking into account a form of agency that is autonomous, meaning that it is not representational. "Political," for many, has come to be associated with representational democracy. It is not that protagonists are not political, but it is a conscious break from a specific form of politics that is related to power over and others, speaking and acting on your behalf, rather than together with you, as social protagonism implies. As Paula from a local assembly explained,

> The experiences have produced profound transformations in people, in the subjectivity of people, in people feeling themselves as actors for the first time in their lives. In the assemblies people from all different backgrounds, of different ages and social situations, have come together to discuss and listen to each other, each person's opinion and voice being valued no more and no less than any other's—this is extremely important, especially considering how the political parties work, which is the opposite. What is being constructed is a new way to do politics. People are the protagonists, the subjects. If the assemblies disappeared tomorrow, it would not be something so serious, because something fundamental has changed in people. People will never again be passive in their lives.[14]

---

14   Paula H, from lesbian, gay, trans movement, interview with Marina Sitrin, Buenos Aires, Argentina, 2003.

AFFECTIVE AND TRUST-BASED CONSTRUCTION

OPENLY DEFINED: Political action and organization based in a relationship of mutual trust, and caring, for the other and the collective.

The current global movements are not only attempting to create the most horizontal and directly democratic spaces, but through new protagonism they are also creating new subjectivities. A part of the grounding for these changing relationships to one another is a base of trust and a growing feeling of care and affect. This is not to be confused with creating intentional communities "outside of society," such as alternative communes, or with creating relationships that are not linked to the idea of acting together for the transformation of society. For example, dancing or cooking together might support a process of building a trusting base for political action, but without action and organizing, it is only dancing or cooking.

In Argentina, the movements began speaking of *política afectiva* (affective politics) as a way of discussing the caring and loving relationships that they felt were growing—and in fact were necessary as a part of the new social construction. They also clarified the challenges to organizing a movement based in love, since many people often do not take the concept of love seriously in a movement. In a macho society, it can be difficult to reach out to new neighbors and workers and ask them to join the "love movement." As Toty reflects below:

> We can have really difficult discussions and disagree, but we all stay part of the organization. We try to love each other. It's difficult. Imagine being in a neighborhood like La Matanza, which is full of really tough men, men who have lived, and still live, a violent, macho life, and we're talking about new loving relationships. No, it isn't easy, not even to talk about, let alone practice. This is part of our changing culture, and as we change, we notice how much we really need to.[15]

Yet even while the challenge is acknowledged, affective politics is still articulated as one of the most important foundations of what is being created. This is especially true for the movements of the unemployed, where participants live in the same neighborhoods, know one another's histories and families, and generally share similar life challenges, from a lack of basic resources to police repression.

While it may seem like an oversimplifica-

---

15   Toty Flores, from the Unemployed Workers Movement (MTD) la Matanza, interview with Marina Sitrin, outside Buenos Aires, Argentina, 2004.

tion to say that if you feel happier with or closer to those with whom you organize, the result will be more social construction and militant activity, this is, in fact, what is seen in practice. Of course, this does not mean one needs to be friends with all people in the movement, or that politics is only done with people with whom one has affection. However, these foundations for organizing have been shown to provide for both more militant action, as has been seen in the recuperated workplaces or the unemployed movements in Argentina. For example, those workplaces where people have the longest history of working together and then reflect on their close relationships to one another, are also the ones that have had the most militant resistance to the police and attempts at evictions. Additionally, people often reflect on how their basis of trust and affect is what helps to keep them going in difficult times of organizing and struggle.

Affect and emotion are too often relegated to the politics of gender and identity, and thus not seen as "serious" theory or as a possibly revolutionary part of politics. This argument denies the fact that responsibility for the other and solidarity are basic conditions of a future society not grounded in capitalist principles. Assigning these characteristics to women and some kind of "maternal sense of responsibility" corresponds to the gendered roles in patriarchal societies, not to a social reality. For example, in the Communal Councils in Venezuela, especially in urban areas, the majority of activists are women. Most women explain their motivation to participate in terms of concern for the future of their kids and other generations. As Libel Espinoza, a young Afro-Venezuelan single mother from the Communal Council "Emiliano Hernández" explained in 2007: "I participate for the sake of my community, my people, for the future of my kids and for my own person."[16] But men active in community organizing argue in exactly the same way. So it's not about "maternal responsibility," but about a social responsibility based on care and affect, human qualities that are necessary to build a new society based on cooperation and mutual aid and not on competition.

Petra Rivas, from the same community outside Caracas as Libel Espinoza, says, "My life has changed . . . I have changed a lot. Above all we became more human, when before everything was from your door to the inside of your house. You did not know what was happening to your neighbor."[17]

"Yesterday night we did an exchange of Christmas gifts in the community," said Jaquelin, "and a lot of people cried because we lived here for so many years without having really anything to do one with one another, even without greeting, and yesterday it was incred-

---

16   Libel Espinoza, interview with Dario Azzellini, Caracas, Venezuela, January 4, 2007.
17   Petra Rivas, Communal Council "Emiliano Hernández," interview with Dario Azzellini, Caracas, Venezuela, January 4, 2007.

ible how we all knew each other, we all talked and hugged."[18] These relationships create and deepen solidarity. The people working more for the community are supported by the community. "I don't get any salary for working in the community," said Jaquelin. "People didn't care about that previously. Now I feel that a lot of people in the community like me and take care of me and my kids. They tell me somehow that I can count on them. That is important."[19]

We cannot write about affect-based politics without acknowledging the role of anger, rage and even hate in politics. It is not only the love or affect for one another and society that impels organizing, but also an anger and hatred for those who make a free society impossible for and toward those who create the conditions of total desperation and crisis for many millions around the world. So while affect is our creative base, it is also tied to a rage against those who work to prevent our freedom.

18   Jaquelin Ávila, Communal Council "Emiliano Hernández," interview with Dario Azzellini, Caracas, Venezuela, December 22, 2006.
19   Jaquelin Ávila, interview with Dario Azzellini, Caracas, Venezuela, December 16, 2008.

AUTOGESTIÓN

OPENLY DEFINED: Autogestión literally means "self-administration," but it usually refers to collective democratic self-management. It can be applied to local communities, workplaces, cultural projects and many other diverse communities and projects.

It was the middle of the night when we arrived in San Luis Acatlán, a town in the southern state of Guerrero, Mexico. San Luís Acatlan is one of ten municipalities formed by sixty-five communities that comprise the region controlled by the "Policía Comunitaria" (Community Police). Most of the communities are indigenous, Mixtec, Tlapanec and Nahua, but there are also seven Mestizo communities that have joined together with the Policía Comunitaria.

Guerrero is one of the poorest, most violent and most repressive states in Mexico. When we arrived, we slept in the central police station of the Policía Comunitaria. The next morning, we were invited to have a coffee with those police on duty. The room had maps and work schedules on the walls, radio equipment on a desk, and few chairs. Outside we could see a dozen policemen in black uniforms with green military T-shirts adorned with the badges of the Policía Comunitaria. Helacio Barrera Q., coordinator of the indigenous community spokespeople welcomed us and explained the origin of the Policía Comunitaria:

"During the 1980s and early 1990s, assaults and armed robberies became more and more frequent in our region. Our people were often robbed when they went from their communities to the market here in the city. Rural workers' organizations and cooperatives were robbed and the members attacked. Women were raped and many people killed. Just one gang operating in the region killed more than seventy people over the years. The government and the official police forces did nothing to help the communities. So the communities decided to organize for their own safety. The communities in this region had started to organize and coordinate in 1989, when we all joined the '500 Years of Indigenous, Black and Popular Resistance' campaign against the 1992 celebrations. After 1992, we maintained the network in the region and became the 'Regional Coordination of Indigenous Authorities of the Mountain and the Costa Chica (Little Coast) of Guerrero.'"[20]

Augustín Barrera C., a founding member of the Policía Comunitaria and head of the police's executive committee reflected: "We knew that organizing our own police would immediately expose us to the repression of the state authorities. So we organized the police secretly, step by step, and on October 14, 1995, we declared simultaneously in

---

20   Helacio Barrera Q., interview with Dario Azzellini, San Luis Acatlán, Mexico, December 9, 2001.

thirty-six communities in three municipalities the existence of the Policía Comunitaria. Then the indigenous authorities informed the public attorney, the army and the regional government that we had founded the Policía Comunitaria."[21]

Helacio Barrera Q. intervenes to say: "And they told us that this is not possible because it is illegal. But we told them we were not asking for permission, we were just informing them what the people had decided in their assembly. And we also told them that the communities decided that the army and the police were no longer allowed to enter our territories without prior permission."

From that moment on, the communities supporting the Policía Comunitaria have been under constant attack by state authorities. The army moved in several times to disarm the police, and community police officers have been arrested under false accusations. These efforts were not able to stop the communities' self-organized police from expanding.

Since the inception of the Community Police, the crime rate decreased 95 percent in the region controlled by the community, which includes approximately 100,000 people. And this was done with only six hundred women and men serving as police officers, armed just with small rifles and without any sophisticated technology or even patrol cars. All police are

---

21 Augustín Barrera C., interview with Dario Azzellini, San Luis Acatlán, Mexico, December 9, 2001.

accountable to the community, and officers are elected by them directly and are only able to serve for a limited time.

Setting up Community Police was just the first step in a process of deepening self-administration—autogestión—enacted by communities. After the people began running their own police force, they found the need to then create their own justice system. They founded one based on re-socialization and not on retribution and vengeance. In the case of minor offenses, if someone breaks the law they are judged on a local level by people who have been elected in local assemblies. If it is a more serious offense, then there is a regional body that judges the accused person.

Under the community justice system, those found guilty are imprisoned in a jail at night; during the day they work on community projects. After a few weeks, the imprisoned person is moved to another community. Each community writes reports about the person, which are then used by the assemblies to decide if he or she should be released earlier. Up until now, most of the people who are apprehended by the Policía Comunitaria, but who are not from the region, chose to be judged by the community justice system rather then being handed over to state authorities. It is also quite common that after these individuals serve their time, they then ask to remain in the communities and to be assigned a specific area of land to work on.

Furthering the development of autogestión that much more, the communities in Guerrero have begun coordinating agricultural production, have built a network of several community radio stations, and have founded an indigenous university.

Guerrero can seem like a far-reaching example of autogestión, but similar autonomous institution building can be found in other parts of Mexico as well, as in the Zapatista communities in Chiapas, and a number of other indigenous communities in Oaxaca, Hidalgo and Veracruz. Each, to differing extents, self-organize the community in a variety of ways through the creation of autonomous collective institutions, ranging from food production and community radio to community governance, as with the Juntas de Buen Gobierno (Good Government Juntas) in Chiapas, as well as medical care, education and alternative adjudication and security processes.

Additionally, there are communities, such as the Nasa in the southwestern highlands of Colombia, who organize an "indigenous guard" through community-based assemblies, and the Regantes[22] in the areas around Cochabamba, Bolivia, who have been organizing their own security forces and autonomous governance since the Water Wars of 2000.

---

22 Literally the "irrigators," the agricultural producers depending on and taking care of irrigation systems. These were parts of the communities that organized autonomously as a result of the "water wars."

Perhaps one of the best-known movements that uses autogestión, along with the Zapatistas, is the Landless Movement (MST) of Brazil. With over one million participants, the MST takes over unused land upon which they collectively use to cultivate crops, develop schools, offer medical care and, to support this process, organize assemblies and administer alternative forms of adjudication and security outside the police and formal institutions of Brazil. Forms of local self-administration are also developing in Venezuela with some Consejos Comunales and Comunas.

So, while it can seem "far off" to think about forming a self-managed community, when one actually begins to explore those that do exist, even with a brief glance at Latin America over the past two decades, one uncovers millions of people already doing just this.

Most often, when one hears of autogestión, it is in the context of workers running their places of work. Examples range from the experiences of cooperatives around the world to the recuperation of workplaces in Argentina and the surrounding region of South America. The meanings of autogestión here range from a self-administered workplace, run with whatever form makes sense and without any organized resistance to the capitalist market, to those in Argentina or Venezuela, which are attempting to facilitate the most horizontal processes possible as well as to push the boundaries of capitalist value exchange in order to create less alienated workplaces, and struggling to barter and exchange with other workplaces based more on needs than on market dictates.

In its essence, autogestión means democratic self-administration. Forms of autogestión exist all over the globe and on all different scales. The Occupy movements, as well as the movements in Spain, Greece and Egypt, have all used autogestión as a way of coordinating within the plazas. And while not perfectly organized, the process of attempting to self-administer a space or community is crucial practice for extending and developing further transformations of society.

Beyond Latin America, many other groups and collectives around the world have experimented with self-administration. Some examples include social centers in Europe, collectives and independent media projects and groups in many parts of the world, and all sorts of alternative education practices, from Free Schools to alternative high school diploma projects in Argentina. In many of these spaces there have been serious attempts to cope with instances of internal conflict. While they are often imperfect, the fact that groups are not only self-organizing and using forms of horizontal democracy but are also trying to solve conflicts as they arise, reflects a growing seriousness with which people are taking autogestión, one that begins to envision a more complete autonomy along with self-administration projects.

AUTONOMY

OPENLY DEFINED: To have the capacity to make decisions about one's own life without having to subordinate these decisions to forces external to the process of self-determination, with a base and limit of the recognition of the autonomy of others.

The language of autonomy is used in the Occupy movements, as well as by many of the movements in Latin America, from the recuperated workplaces and unemployed movements in Argentina, to the Zapatista communities in Mexico and many of the grassroots organizations in Venezuela. All use the term autonomy to distinguish themselves from movements, groups or organizations subordinated to external interest, including the state, political parties and other groups and institutions.

Autonomy reflects the politics of self-organization, *autogestión* and direct participation. In essence, the concept of autonomy, as people in the movements are using it, is a "do it ourselves" approach to politics and social organization. As Maba from the Unemployed Workers Movement of Solano, outside Buenos Aires, explains, "Autonomy, direct democracy, and *horizontalidad* are built. We don't say, today we're all autonomists.... It's a process."[23]

23   Maba, from the MTD Solano, interview with Marina Sitrin, outside Buenos Aires, Argentina, 2004

Emilio, from the Tierra del Sur neighborhood assembly, occupied building, and community center in Buenos Aires, points out a fundamental contradiction: "The idea that we can be non-capitalistic within a capitalist system is a fallacy, because capitalism intersects our lives all the time. What we can do, however, is build and create different things without following the logic of the capitalist system. Autonomy is a tool for gaining our freedom."[24]

Osvaldo León, a worker in the Venezuelan aluminum factory Alcasa and an activist for worker control, makes an important point: "The forms of action that have persisted over time are mainly the ones [that come from] the people themselves, having autonomy and independence, because they are based on experience and history."[25] Movements understand autonomy as a process of construction related to self-administration, one that reflects a refusal to follow capitalist logic.

The idea of autonomy can be traced back to many struggles in history. After the Italian *autonomia* movement in the 1960s and '70s, and the autonomous movements in central and northern Europe in the 1980s, it was from the 1994 Zapatista uprising in Mexico that the ideas of autonomy regained widespread interest. Zapatista philosophy and practice—

24 Emilio, from Tierra del Sur assembly, interview with Marina Sitrin, Jujuy, Argentina, 2004.
25 Osvaldo León, Colectivo Control Obrero Alcasa, interview with Dario Azzellini, Ciudad Guayana, Venezuela, April 21, 2008.

Zapatismo—have many orientations and practices in common with other non-indigenous autonomist movements and links itself to them. The Zapatistas raise autonomy in an indigenous context, not as a concept of territorial separation but as the right to decide and exercise their own forms of social, political and economic organization. The Zapatistas set up their own form of self-government, one which has evolved over time into the constitution of "autonomous municipalities." They have set up their own primary schools, health system and regional planning system for agricultural production, as well as a network of community-controlled radio stations that broadcast in the indigenous languages Chol, Tojolabal, Tzeltal and Tzotzil. The new structures are based on the culture, experiences and collective decisions of the Zapatista communities. It's not about folkloric habits but about creating something new based on one's own reality, needs and wishes. In the Zapatista schools, to give an example, the classes are bilingual, so the children learn Spanish, but also learn in their own language, and the learning materials are also based on the reality the people live and not state-imposed textbooks that refer to a different history, lifestyle and culture.

As a part of the creation of autonomous ways of being, not only are the movements creating ways to meet their basic necessities as much as possible, but they are also finding ways to often resolve conflicts without the state and police. That does not mean autonomy is like autarchy, a total independence from everything and everybody else, but that the decisions are not subordinated to other forces. This entails an increasingly complicated relationship to the state. The problem is that the capitalist state is based on territorial hegemony and homogenization. It sometimes allows parallel structures, but usually if they do not challenge its absolute authority. As soon as autonomous self-organization questions state power (potentially or concretely), it becomes the object of repression, violence and destruction. Ezequiel from the Asamblea Cid Campeador, a neighborhood assembly in Buenos Aires, explains:

The state exists, it's there, and it won't leave even if you ignore it. It will come to look for you however much you wish that it didn't exist. I believe that the assemblies and movements are beginning to notice that something important is being forgotten. . . . We began to think of a strategy for constructing an alternative autonomous power, forgetting the state, but now we see it isn't so simple.[26]

Also discussing autonomous construction and the relationship to the state, Wilson Moya, a fifty-year-old car mechanic living in the Magallanes de Catia shantytowns of Caracas and active in his local Consejo Comunal, an

---

26 Ezequiel, from the assembly Cid Campeador, interview with Marina Sitrin, Buenos Aires, Argentina, 2003.

assembly-based form of local self-government in Venezuela, reflected, "This is just the beginning—you will see, the only thing existing here will be the Consejos Comunales; we are constructing autonomy, we already have a certain autonomy, and we will make this work better and better."[27] Local autonomy in Venezuela is not being built in isolation from the state or as a "counterweight" to it, but through a complicated network of self-administration, often overcoming the divisions between the political, social and economic, and attempting to turn the state, in its known form, into one that is unnecessary in the long term. But even in a situation like Venezuela's, with a leftist government officially orientated toward supporting the movements and self-organization, the situation is contradictory and complex. There is an inherent logic of the state and institutions of power to control social processes and reproduce and sustain their own hierarchies of power. Hence the movements exist as a constant struggle to build autonomy and not be subordinated to the state and its institutions, with the movements having to constantly exercise pressure to force the institutions to act in the way previously agreed to: following the will of the people. This struggle, as with all the struggles for autonomy, is open-ended and still to be determined.

---

27   Wilson Moya, Consejo Comunal "Emiliano Hernández,"
interview with Dario Azzellini, Caracas, Venezuela, January 9, 2007.

"TODOS SOMOS . . ."

OPENLY DEFINED: Voiced as a slogan or chant, "*Todos somos . . .*" translates directly as "We all are . . . ," and expresses an identification with others, often different from you, as in "We are all Trayvon Martin" or "We are all Troy Davis" or "We are all Bradley Manning." The phrase conveys a strong sense of solidarity between struggles and movements in various situations.

One of the characteristics of the ways these new movements are attempting to organize people and movements around the world, both internally and in relationship to other groups, is a base of acceptance and recognition. This means not only the acceptance of one another and the appreciation of diversities, as opposed to homogenization, but also that we see ourselves in the other and that we also see the other in ourselves. It is a linking of struggles, not a hierarchizing of them. This does not mean that there are not power differentials, or that all people experience life in the same way (for example, with oppression or without access to resources), but that only in recognizing all of these diversities and differentials, and not giving power-based priority to one over the other, are we able to create an emancipatory base from which to organize together.

Voiced as a slogan, "Todos somos . . ." has been used in different movements throughout history.

For example, many guerrilla forces and liberation movements have expressed this concept through the tradition of militants picking up the name of a fallen comrade. In Latin American human rights movements such as the Madres de la Plaza de Mayo in Argentina, many refer to those who were murdered by the dictatorship in the "we" form, a sort of collective identification with "our" children who were killed, or a way of saying that those who were killed are also us, as seen with the phrase "*El otro soy yo*" (I am the other).

The use of "Todos somos . . ." regained force and spread around the world in the aftermath of the Zapatista uprising which began on January 1, 1994. Support for the indigenous rebellion was so strong in Mexico and internationally that the Mexican government did not risk using militarily force to crush the insurgent communities after the short period of combat had ended. Instead, the government developed a massive propaganda campaign against the Zapatistas and in particular against their most charismatic spokesperson, Subcomandante Marcos, publicizing his alleged previous identity and attacking him in an attempt to damage his image. When this campaign began, throughout Mexico and then the world, people took up the slogan "*Todos Somos Marcos.*" In 1995 the Mexican press joined the government's campaign to discredit the Zapatistas, and again Marcos in particular, and accused him of being gay. Marcos responded with the following statement.

Yes, Marcos is gay. Marcos is gay in San Francisco, Black in South Africa, an Asian in Europe, a Chicano in San Ysidro, an anarchist in Spain, a Palestinian in Israel, a Mayan Indian in the streets of San Cristóbal, a Jew in Germany, a Gypsy in Poland, a Mohawk in Quebec, a pacifist in Bosnia, a single woman on the Metro at 10 p.m., a peasant without land, a gang member in the slums, an unemployed worker, an unhappy student and, of course, a Zapatista in the mountains.

Marcos is all the exploited, marginalized, oppressed minorities resisting and saying, "Enough!" He is every minority who is now beginning to speak and every majority that must shut up and listen. He is every untolerated group searching for a way to speak. Everything that makes power and the good consciences of those in power uncomfortable—this is Marcos.[28]

The idea that we are all Marcos, together with the way Marcos described himself—that he/we are all one another, and particularly the most oppressed, marginalized and vulnerable— opened for a new ways of discussing identity,

28 Quoted in "Farewell to the End of History: Organization and Vision in Anti-Corporate Movements" by Naomi Klein, from *The Socialist Register*, 2002, London: Merlin Press, 1–14

difference, social relationships and responsibilities to one another. This understanding was already in practice in the indigenous Zapatista communities, but the statement by Marcos served to spread it far beyond Mexico. This idea does not come from a place of solidarity in the old, traditional sense of doing for the other, but in each of us seeing ourselves in the oppressed other—in actually being the other—and the other being us. And around the world, people in struggle started to use the slogan "*Todos somos Zapatistas*" to indicate not only their solidarity with the Zapatistas, but also their identification with concepts and practices of the Zapatista movement. The slogan "Todos somos . . ." was soon adapted to other contexts and situations around the globe.

A MOVEMENT OF MOVEMENTS

OPENLY DEFINED: The heterogeneous mixture of groups and movements, with different causes, forms of organization, tactics and strategies, networking together against neoliberal globalization.

Over one thousand people are sitting very close together on the floor of a high school gymnasium. At first glance the scene appears chaotic, but if one could gaze down from above, a very different picture would emerge—one would see the shape and design of a bicycle wheel. There is an open space in the very center where five people are standing, and then around them is a circle of perhaps sixty people, and then behind each of the sixty there are anywhere from a dozen to a few dozen people sitting in a line.

We are in a donated space in a working-class Latino neighborhood in Washington, D.C. All have gathered in this spokes council to discuss how to shut down the International Monetary Fund and World Bank meetings in the upcoming days. The energy is high, jubilant even, as the five people in the center, the facilitators, try to begin the assembly. Finally they shout out, "If you can hear the sound of my voice, clap once." Some people clap. "If you can hear the sound of my voice, clap twice." More people clap, and by the time they get to three times, the point has been made and the group is quieter.

The assembly begins with the facilitators explaining the modified rules of consensus that the spokes council will be using. After questions and clarifications, it is time for each spoke, that person sitting in the center circle, with the dozens behind them, to introduce their affinity group or cluster. A cluster is a group of more than two affinity groups that decide to work together on a particular action, and thus merge into one for the sake of a spokes council. The person speaking, the "spoke," is not a "representative" but merely the "voice" of those behind them. The introductions begin. People have gathered from all over the east coast of the United States, many in temporary affinity groups, to come together for this specific action with an agreed-

upon tactic or strategy. Affinity groups for the sake of the action have all sorts of creative names, and their desired actions range over a great deal of territory. Then there are those who come from organizations, who for the purpose of participating in the spokes council use the affinity group model of organization. These groups range from religious organizations to community-based groups. There are also a few labor groups represented, as well as schools and university-based affinity groups. After the introductions, the groups go around again and share what they have decided so far they will do on the streets on the days of actions. Again the responses range from those who will dance and sing and then move if the police come, to others who will lock arms and block roads, risking arrest, to others who will block roads until the police arrive, then disperse to another location to begin a new blockade. The forms of action the different groups, organizations and actors want to use and the risks they are willing to take differ a great deal, but they decide together to accept the legitimacy of all practices and share a common goal.

These one thousand people, who then turned into tens of thousands on the days of action against the International Monetary Fund and World Bank, are a movement of movements.

The framework of a movement of movements is often used to describe movements that share a similar foundation in what they are for and against, and—most important—that are all networked in one way or another, usually for global days of action, campaigns, information sharing and international *encuentros*. Most recently this concept, though not the exact phrase, has been used in the new global movements to refer to any individual or group that identifies with the 99% or Real Democracy, those who join encampments, participate in assemblies and position themselves with the movements. There is no strict politics one needs to subscribe to; rather, it is an open sense where many with the same general rejections of policies causing crisis around the globe can find a common space upon which to create new relationships. Similarly, people speak of the new movements, or the movements since 2010, or group them geographically, e.g., the Arab Spring, the European Summer and the U.S. Fall, and while each place is quite distinct, the general nature of the movements, responding to the crisis and doing so in a similar way, has created the sense of a movement of movements that we refer to here.

Movement of movements is a term that emerged with the anti-globalization movement, and the gatherings organized against international political, economic, military and financial summits around the world. The movement of movements points to the bringing together of organizations, initiatives, groups and collectives in a struggle for a common goal, e.g., against neoliberal globalization. As a consequence of the diversity of participants, ranging anywhere from anarchists, socialists and communists to spiritual pacifists, ecologists, migrants, feminists and labor groups, there is a wide diversity of views with regard to such things as organization, politics, structure and strategy. The participants differ in their analysis of the causes and possible solutions of the problem, and even in the steps to take and means to use to bring forward change. But they come together and agree on a common agenda of mobilizations and a shared frame of mutually accepted forms of action. The global dimension, as well as the commitment to working together despite differences, characterizes the movement of movements as a new phenomenon.

At the same time that the concept of the movement of movements refers to most everyone who chooses to work together on common mobilizations around a broader issue, this loose definition does not reflect all aspects of the movement of movements. The global justice movement mobilized hundreds of thousands of people across North America and many millions around Europe, Latin America and Asia. But the people mobilized and the movements coming together for campaigns did not simply cohere out of some kind of natural process, and similarly, the mobilizations did not just happen on their own. Behind the mobilizations there were, and always are, smaller networks sharing affinity around political vision, forms of organization and the means of struggle.

These initiatives strategically constructed the larger campaigns and mobilizations and built a sort of backbone to them. One can find many different types of global networks, such as unions and union activists, progressive spiritual communities, radical intellectuals, and so on, but under the surface of the common mobilizations, the most significant networking elements were the self-organized grassroots groups, collectives and organizations. Most of these groups and collectives were against hierarchy and political party structures, and were largely anti-authoritarian in spirit, if not in practice.

These groups coordinated in hundreds of cities and towns, and networked with others like them around their country and the globe, and often set the frame for the common activities of the movement of movement as a whole, including how to work together and make decisions. Among some of the more important globally organized networks were the international land workers' organization, Via Campesina, and People's Global Action (PGA). In Europe, there was a strong network with the participation of the Disobedients' movement in Italy, Reclaim the Streets and others in Great Britain, and what later turned into the coordination the Interventionist Left (*Interventionistische Linke*) in Germany as well as groups and organizations throughout most of the European countries with similar perspectives on organization, practices and goals.

During the 1999 anti-WTO Seattle protests in the United States, it was the Direct Action Network (DAN) that coordinated the actions early on, but also facilitated the participation of hundreds of other groups, organizations and unions to be able to all work together on the days of action, a movement of movements of sorts. After Seattle, dozens of Direct Action Networks sprang up around the United States, coordinating with one another through the Continental DAN. The way each group organized was decided locally, but the implicit consistencies were anti-capitalist politics, a basis of non-hierarchy and a focus on changing social relationships. The use of the consensus process was also fairly consistent with the organizing movement of movements.

TERRITORY AND SPACE

OPENLY DEFINED: Technically, "territory" is a geographical place with defined boundaries, whereas "space" is a set of constructed social relations (social, economic, political, cultural) within a certain territory. But the growing commodification of territories by capitalism has raised the need to claim territories for the construction of spaces with alternative values and practices. And that has generated different, sometimes contradictory uses of the terms territory and space in different movements. Regardless of the different ways the terms are used, the meanings are quite similar, and are being articulated more and more around the globe.

Ayelen, a participant in Spain's 15M movement, speaking about the use of the space in the Plaza del Sol, commented, "These were times that you'd go to the plaza on one day, and then when you returned on the next day seven hundred new things had come up. I remember one day I got there and I was told, 'They built a vegetable garden,' and I said, 'A vegetable garden!?' And yes, it was there, *in the fountain* of the Plaza del Sol of Madrid! And suddenly there was a nursery, and a library, and . . . it was fascinating. There was this thing about doing. Doing, doing, and doing."[29]

In a 2003 conversation, Martín K. from the Argentine neighborhood assemblies of Colegiales, Buenos Aires, said: "Since there are no institutions, not even a club, a church, or anything, the assembly meets on any corner, and even in the street. When this new form of politics emerges it establishes a new territory, or spatiality. . . . In the beginning, the assembly consisted of people from all walks of life, ranging from the housewife who declared, 'I am not political,' to the typical party hack.

---

29 Ayelen, 15M movement, interview with Dario Azzellini and Marina Sitrin, Madrid, Spain, January 22, 2012.

But there was a certain sensibility. I don't know what to call it, something affective. . . . It's as if we live in flux, moving at a certain speed, like little balls bouncing all about, and then suddenly, the assembly is our intention to establish a bay, to momentarily pause time and space, and to say, 'Let us think about how to avoid being dragged and bounced about, and simultaneously attempt to build something new ourselves.'"[30]

The Zapatistas have made the autonomy of indigenous territories in Chiapas one of the central points of their struggle, and they have declared the territory in which the Zapatista construction of a different and democratically self-administered society takes place as "*territorio zapatista*," words we see written on large roadside signs when we enter the regions of Chiapas where the Zapatista communities are based. Sometimes they relate to other "rebel territories" in their process of construction and sometimes to the whole territory of Mexico (meaning the people within the boundaries of Mexico), regardless of the level of conflict or cooperation with the governments in power. Over the last two decades, the "demarcation of indigenous territory" has become a core question of indigenous struggles around the globe. In these territories, claimed by dispossessed indigenous groups, they have begun processes

---

30   Martin K, from the Assembly of Colegiales, interview with Marina Sitrin, Buenos Aires, Argentina, 2003.

of self-administration, under their own rules, based on their own cultures.

The relationship of movements to territory has been important in urban areas for the construction of alternative social relationships as well as for the interruption of capitalist business as usual. The unemployed workers' movements in Argentina began as a protest, demanding an unemployment subsidy from the state, but the movement transformed into something different. Not having a workplace within which to base the struggle, the protest took the form of a *piquete*, a blockade. Bridges or major intersections turned into spaces of struggle, with the intention of shutting down major transportation arteries. Along with blockades, they began to create horizontal assemblies. The assemblies opened conversations about what to do next, but also facilitated an entire infrastructure of food, health care, media and child care and began to refer to this space as free "*territorio*." From these new territories on the *piquete*, the same practices were expanded into the neighborhoods, often taking over land and building homes, growing crops and raising animals together, and generating a wide range of projects in areas from clothes production to health care. These were always organized with horizontal assemblies, creating a new community and a new territory.

Andrés Antillano from the grassroots Urban Land Committees in Caracas, Venezuela, explains the changing concept of territory and space from within the poor neighborhoods (barrios):

"Considering the effects of capitalist society, the barrios express alternative values, because they are a product of the struggle of the people. And how to build the space in the barrio is an ongoing controversial issue. The struggle against segregation is also a struggle for the right to the city. . . . The question of territory is not just a spatial question. For us it is a question of identity, of community, it is an affective question, it is the place where the people know each other, marry their neighbor, build common histories, push forward common proposals and projects. For us, so to say, the territory, the community is not only a place, it is a political, a politicized, subject, we live all together. As a consequence, the question of territory is very important to us. Just to let you know, territory for us is an area of about two hundred families, and we ourselves define what exactly is the territory of the neighborhood we are talking about."[31]

Used in the context of movements, territory and space are about the construction of autonomous community. And "community" is not a given "place"; it is a set of social relations that has to be built actively. Trust, affect,

---

31   Andrés Antillano, from the grassroots Urban Land Committees in Caracas, interview with Dario Azzellini, Caracas, Venezuela, January 25, 2007.

care and responsibility for the other are the base of this set of social relations, and the community is also strengthening these values. In the process, those people involved change—the development of social relationships is dynamic and place based. When interviewed, activists of Communal Councils in Venezuela often describe their personal transformation as having become "more human." Jaquelin Ávila, from the Consejo Comunal "Emiliano Hernández," put it this way in 2008:

"The most important thing I learned is that my human sensibility has been woken up. I participated in going from house to house to see who urgently needs a new house because the shack they are living in represents a high risk. I have been in houses where I came out crying after I saw the human misery that existed. . . . My life changed, and as a person, I grew a lot." [32]

From the indigenous movements reclaiming territories in Latin America to the neighborhood movements from big cities such as Buenos Aires and Caracas, to new movements in Europe and the United States taking over the plazas and founding social centers, concrete territory plays a central role in the construction of new social relationships. Even if the exam-

32 Jaquelin Ávila, from the Consejo Comunal "Emiliano Hernández", interview with Dario Azzellini, Caracas, Venezuela, December 16, 2008.

ples are very different from one to the other, they can be traced back to a common origin and a common sensibility. Because advancing capitalism has commodified more and more territories and spaces, there is a need to reclaim them to build social relationships that are not subjected to commodification.

While for more than five hundred years indigenous people have been mainly in retreat from advancing commodification and subjugation, a point was reached where they could not withdraw anymore or go anywhere without again being dispossessed. In order to survive they have no other choice but to claim territories in which they can live the way they choose. And in the poor urban neighborhoods, especially in shantytowns, which are often not even officially recognized as existing urban territories, the inhabitants claim the territory and defend their own history of sociality and struggle, as well as the concrete process of constructing communities against commodification, institutionalization or criminal cooptation. Taking over public space, as with the assemblies on the streets in Argentina, or the occupied plazas in the United States or Spain, or the creation of "social centers" throughout Europe, is a consequence of the neoliberal politics of the last decades, which have been privatizing public space and tying a person's access to cultural and social participation to their ability to consume. So the creation of new social relations and spaces in which everyone can participate and socialize, regardless of his or her buying power, needs the appropriation of territories in which this can happen.

MAY DAY

OPENLY DEFINED: May Day is International Workers' Day. It is celebrated every year by tens of millions of people in most countries around the world. It originated with the struggle for the eight-hour workday, and in particular with the experience of the police repression against workers in Chicago in 1886. In the 1980s, more diverse movements began organizing around May Day, and since 2001, the concept has shifted to one not only celebrating workers, but also standing up for immigrant rights, for social justice and against capitalist globalization and war.

More than one hundred people fit into a union hall meant for fifty. We are planning actions and events for May Day 2012 in New York City. The air is stale, but the energy high. The room is filled with Occupy movement participants, immigrant rights groups, progressive labor unions—and those from labor not representing their unions, or without unions but identifying as labor—and a few people from neighborhood workers' centers and other community-based groups. The form of organization the May Day planning has taken is a spokes council (inspired by the global justice movement and, it is rumored, also the Spanish anarchists of the 1930s). It is a directly democratic form of organization that can be used so that decisions are made, or ideas shared, among people speaking who are already involved in some form of organizing, reflected in things such as working groups, affinity groups or organizations. No more than one person from each group has a formal "voice," though everyone has "ears," and contributes to what their voice, technically a "spoke," says to the group. There are often conversations whispered up and down the line of spokes to figure out what the "voice" should say, based on what others in the group feel and think. Consensus or agreement is reached in each group before ideas are shared and proposed.

The organizing behind May Day 2012 was just one of countless examples of a current practice that has numerous antecedents, though many of those organizing may not know the various histories. While May Day began as a day of struggle that mobilized all sorts of workers—immigrants, leftists, socialists, communists, anarcosyndicalists and anarchists—after World War II, particularly in Europe and the United States, it became characterized more by reformist union marches. In 1958, the U.S. government even tried to hijack the day and redefine it as "Loyalty Day," attempting to physically obstruct mobilizations. With the decline of the industrial labor force in the late 1970s in the global North, May

Day seemed to wane as a point of reference for movements, especially in the global North.

In recent decades, however, instead of continuing to lose importance, May Day has begun to be re-signified by the movements and has again become a center of massive mobilization. One thread of May Day re-appropriation can be found in the "Revolutionary May Day" demonstrations in Germany and parts of northern Europe. They trace back to May 1, 1987, when police stormed a peaceful street festival organized by revolutionary collectives and neighborhood organizations in the Kreuzberg neighborhood of Berlin, an area characterized by strong immigrant and leftist populations. Radical activists and inhabitants of Kreuzberg started to fight back against police attacks, setting up barricades and burning police cars. The battle turned into an urban uprising, which eventually forced the police out of the neighborhood for the night. That night the streets in the heart of Kreuzberg were filled with massive street parties, while simultaneously there was looting of shops and grocery stores. The Kreuzberg uprising became a symbol, and ever since, "Revolutionary May Day" demonstrations are held in Kreuzberg, often with some 20,000 participants. The police mobilize for every one, and repression and skirmishes almost always occur. Over the years "Revolutionary May Day" has spread to other cities in Germany and throughout northern Europe.

Another appropriation of May 1 by the more recent movements is EuroMayDay.[33] Euro-MayDay began in 2005 in dozens of European cities, including Milan, Naples, Berlin, Hamburg, Paris, Helsinki, Seville-Malaga, Lisbon, Vienna, Maribor, Zurich, Copenhagen, and Liège, and then spread to other cities around the world, such as Tokyo and Toronto, losing its prefix "Euro." The EuroMayDay Parade emerged from the global justice movement in October 2004, during an autonomous event organized parallel to the European Social Forum. The basic idea was to unify the struggles of precarious workers and migrants for social rights and the freedom of movement across borders, as well as to create a trans-European network for mobilizations, beyond what was then a single day of mobilization focus. The first coordinated EuroMayDay was held in 2005. Its origins go back to 2001 in Milan, Italy, when an alliance of labor activists of precarious workers, Rank-and-File Union Committees (CUB), squatted social centers and migrant organizations unified efforts for a May Day of the "precarious." The term "precarious" refers to all people living with income and work insecurity, having uneven or no access to social services and/or being subjected to repressive migration laws.

---

33   May Day, written as MayDay or mayday, referred also to the international emergency call "Mayday Mayday Mayday" (from French *m'aider*, short for *venez m'aider*, "come help me").

To understand today's May Day is to see the diversity of the subjectivities engaged in it as an enrichment of the struggle. Seen from this perspective, the concept of unity is quite different from the concept prevailing in traditional workers' and leftist organizations, where unity is based more on homogenization. The diversity is often expressed in the form of a parade that mixes joyous celebration with direct actions, such as temporary occupations of institutions, expropriation of food and other goods from chain stores, and the use of public transport without paying. The parade, in turn, draws upon the tactics of the global justice movement where joy and celebration were core, as with groups such as Reclaim the Streets and the Pink Block. Some of the MayDay networks became places where precarious workers, migrants and other workers came for support around particular issues, struggles and actions not necessarily related to May 1 actions. The rubric of MayDay spread, and its networks became central to organizing around issues such as the struggles and protests of precarious workers, including those in call centers or short-term contract workers in the service industries, as well as struggles against deportation and detention centers, against copyright and for general access to services understood as commons. The different MayDays around Europe met regularly for discussion and coordination and made transnational calls for demonstrations.

Elizabeth Knafo and MPA, Brooklyn

As of 2010 this form of organization began to shift, and while they still exist, they have also again begun to change form.

The practices that grew out of MayDay spread beyond the mobilizations for May 1 with, for example, satirical inventions such as the popular icon of "Saint Precarious" or the "Precarious Superheroes," appearing in other campaigns and movements. The "Precarious Superheroes" stand for the amount of "super-hero capability" precarious workers must have in their jobs and lives. Dressed in colorful fantasy clothing like traditional superheroes, the "Precarious Superheroes" have been participating in demonstrations and direct actions. For example, in Hamburg, Germany, "Precarious Superheroes" expropriated expensive food from a luxury store and distributed it for free to unemployed, homeless and low-income workers in the days preceding May Day 2006.

In the United States, May Day 2006 was again placed on the national agenda as a day of struggle. Migrant communities and organizations called for a May 1 national boycott and in some places a "Day Without an Immigrant," with many millions of immigrants and migrant workers participating across the country, from the major cities to small towns. In Los Angeles, close to one million people took to the streets. In New York, a march of tens of thousands— perhaps hundreds of thousands—took streets and bridges as people made their way from

Brooklyn to Manhattan. Solidarity actions were organized in Mexico as well, with a "Nothing Gringo Boycott," intending to show cross-border solidarity with migrant communities. Since 2006, immigrant rights and power have been a core part of every May Day in the United States.

In 2008, the West Coast dockworkers' union (International Longshore and Warehouse Union, or ILWU) called for a May Day strike in the United States, demanding "an immediate end to the war and occupation in Iraq and Afghanistan and the withdrawal of U.S. troops from the Middle East." Approximately 30,000 members, along with tens of thousands of other supporters, shut down the port that day. Taken together, these forces have reasserted the question of class, as a possible militant force, into May Day.

While in most of the global South, May Day never lost its appeal as a significant day for struggle, with militant resistance as well as joyous celebrations, in the global North it is only in the past decade that it has been increasingly reclaimed, from below, as the day of the struggle for dignity of the oppressed, silenced and marginalized. May Day is also being recuperated as a day of joy, of celebrating together the vast diversity of protagonists and participants, and of the changes to come—it is a moment when one catches a glimpse of tomorrow. What began as a recuperation of May Day's radical tradition by activists of political groups and precarious workers, has increasingly turned into a broader movement, with May Day as a central symbol.

The planning for May Day 2012 in New York was a combination of all of the above. There were traditional workers' unions, especially the more progressive segments, immigrant rights organizations and communities, and many working groups from Occupy. The Occupy group Mutual Aid provided many free goods and services, including food from local farmers and producers, child care, tutoring and medical consultations. The Messaging group worked on getting the movement's perspective communicated by creating media and interacting with mainstream media. Direct Action carried out plans to shut down major road arteries, doing so theatrically and with joy. The Plus Brigades planned direct action as clown blocks. The Art and Culture working group organized so that people could publicly create art on May Day, and helped make the action beautiful.

The conversation about striking, what it means to be a worker, and even the meaning of "stopping business as usual" was another powerful intervention made by the May Day planning around the globe. Discussions about the meaning of "strike" expanded beyond action by traditional factory workers to include precarious workers, using the language of precarity. It also brought more centrally into the conversation the immigration and migration statuses of the possible participants, and the risks people might face if they were to strike in the traditional sense.

While some workers in the United States did strike, many others took the spirit of the idea of a strike broadly—striking with a way of being and doing things. Celebrating the holiday of May Day and resisting together, but doing so in a multitude of ways. People organized marches, parades, music and art as well as ongoing popular education and workshops. The events of May Day 2012 began first thing in the morning, and with tens of thousands of participants in New York alone, lasted all day and into the night. The day closed after a transit workers' union rally was held, with an assembly of many hundreds of people reflecting on the day, the state of the movement and the many possible futures.

The influence of the global South and our own history on our current practices becomes clearer with each movement that organizes and each massive event coordinated. It is not linear, perhaps, but nonetheless, many aspects of the past twenty years can be seen in the shifting nature of May Day in the New York and U.S. May Day. How did this happen? One of our many questions . . .

POLITICS OF WALKING
AND PROCESS

OPENLY DEFINED: Politics based on an open-ended, ever-evolving collective process of social construction that defines and redefines the means of emancipation through constant discussion and debate among participants.

"What are your demands?"

"We don't use the framework of demands."

"But what does Occupy want?"

"We are organizing spaces where people can come together and, using real democracy, discuss what we might want, and find ways of making that happen."

"But you must have demands to be taken seriously."

"We have only been gathering together for a few months, and there are now hundreds of thousands of people across the country coming together in assemblies to discuss what we want."

"SO, what do you want? What is your program for society?"

"We have begun to do what we want, which is to come together in our towns, neighborhoods, schools, workplaces and communities to create new relationships together, using the tools of horizontal democracy. And in the process of meeting one another we have begun to work on projects in common, not asking anyone to do things for us, but doing them ourselves and together. This does not

mean that we do not want many things from the state; in fact, many of us see all of what they have as rightfully ours, but we are not writing a ten-point plan for society telling people how to change things.

"Perhaps as time goes on, as we continue to create together, we will have demands, but for now we are beginning the process of discovery, democracy and collective action. It is not about a final point or objective, but the process of coming together and struggling together where we will find our many paths. It is on this walk together that we discover the path, creating it as we go."

The concept of walking and questioning, or making the road as one walks, while questioning, has been used throughout history. More recently, the Zapatistas popularized the idea, and then the concept was carried around the world, movement to movement. A story that has been told and retold throughout the Mayan communities of Chiapas, Mexico, is called the "Story of Questions." This story has now been passed along, read and performed at countless global gatherings and *encuentros* everywhere. It captures the spirit of questioning as we walk. It also captures the social and collective necessity of the walk. It conveys our need for one another, and that only through relating and listening to each other can we discover our walk. Here is a selection of the story, as retold by Subcomandante Marcos in 2001:

Many stories ago, when the first gods—those who made the world— were still circling through the night, there were these two other gods—Ik'al and Votán.

The two were only one. When one was turning himself around, the other would show himself, and when the other one was turning himself around, the first one would show himself. They were opposites. One was light like a May morning at the river. The other was dark like night of cold and cave.

They were the same thing. They were one, these two, because one made the other. But they would not walk themselves, staying there always, these two gods who were one without moving.

"What should we do then?" the two of them asked.

"Life is sad enough as it is," they lamented, the two who were one in staying without moving.

"Night never passes," said Ik'al.

"Day never passes," said Votán.

"Let's walk," said the one who was two.

"How?" asked the other.

"Where?" asked the one.

And they saw that they had moved a little, first to ask how, then to ask where. The one who was two became very happy when the one saw that they were moving themselves a little. Both of them wanted to move at the same time, but they couldn't do it themselves.

"How should we do it then?"

And one would come around first and then the other and they would move just a little bit more and they realized that they could movie if one went first, then the other. So they came to an agreement that—in order to move—one had to move first, then the other. So they started walking and now no one remembers who started walking first because at the time they were so happy just to be moving. . . .

And they were going to start walking when their answer to choose the long road brought another question—"Where does this road take us?" They took a long time to think about the answer and the two who were one got the bright idea that only by walking the long road were they going to know where the road took them. If they remained where they were, they were never going to know where the long road leads.[34]

---

34 There are countless versions of this story. The one included here is the one most widespread in English, due mainly to Subcomandante Marcos retelling it and having it translated first on the Internet and then in the book *Questions and Swords: Folktales of the Zapatista Revolution* (Cinco Puntos Press, 2001).

The global movements, particularly since 2011, organize based in a very similar spirit of walking and questioning, not trying to force everybody to sign up to the same program and master plan on how to make the program reality. The practice is rather to open democratic spaces for the convergence of ideas and practices. As with the Zapatistas, and many of the movements in Latin America over the last two decades, there has been a real break in particular forms of organizing, ones that are hierarchical and have the answers and the "program" predetermined.[35] Instead, what movements are creating is a multiplicity of paths toward an ever-changing end. Many see the path as an integral part of this changing end.

Not to be mistaken, these are very concrete paths, such as the taking over of hundreds of workplaces and pushing the boundaries of capitalist value production in places such as Argentina and Brazil. The projects are concrete and militant; it is only that the "goal" is a multiplicity and one discovered as people struggle and create together. Another example of the end as a pro-

---

35   In this context it is important to underline that democracy and horizontalism do not mean that every single space and situation is organized following these principles, but that first the process of horizontal democracy opens the conversation about what forms are most appropriate. And in certain cases it has been found that it is not possible to always maintain horizontal decisions. For example, the EZLN is a military structure that is generally subordinated to the democratic decisions of the supporting Zapatista base communities. But as a military structure it also needs a chain of command and cannot submit every step and action to an assembly. The same can be said about certain production processes that might decide horizontally that they need a chain of command.

cess is in Venezuela. People in the communities and movements there refer to what is taking place as a "process." While there is a stated "goal" of creating "socialism of the twenty-first century," it is not an ideology predetermining a certain structure or form. It is a search, a "work in progress," based on a set of values that include solidarity, mutuality, community, equality, self-administration, democracy, freedom and so on. The motor behind what is developed and constructed is meant to be the neighborhoods, communities and workplaces; thus the meaning of this twenty-first-century socialism is an ever-changing one, and one that in itself is also the walk. This does not mean that there are not different and conflicting visions of what should be done or how, or that there are not people who have more power to impose themselves than others do. But the idea is to have an open process of creation and understand even deep structural change such as revolution is not an act but a process.

No one is able to tell where the various directly democratic and participatory movements for change around the globe will go on their walk. That is to be determined. But without a doubt they have created and are creating huge and exciting social laboratories, spaces of participation and creation of the new. The future is unwritten. . . .

Caminando preguntamos. . . .

ABOUT THE AUTHORS

 DARIO AZZELLINI is an activist, writer and film maker. His latest film is *Comuna Under Construction* about local self government in Venezuela, and latest book, together with Immanuel Ness, *Ours to Master and to Own: Workers' Control from the Commune to the Present*. He is a lecturer at the Institute for Sociology at the Johannes Kepler University in Austria. (www.azzellini.net)

 MARINA SITRIN is a participant in the Occupy movements, the editor of *Horizontalism: Voices of Popular Power in Argentina* and author of *Everyday Revolutions: Horizontalism and Autonomy in Argentina*. She is a postdoctoral fellow at the CUNY Graduate Center's Committee on Globalization and Social Change. (www.marinasitrin.com)

RECENT AND FORTHCOMING FROM ZUCCOTTI PARK PRESS

OCCUPY
by Noam Chomsky
$9.95

TAKING BROOKLYN BRIDGE
by Stuart Leonard
Bilingual edition (English/ Spanish)
$5

MESSAGE TO THE MOVEMENT
by Mumia Abu-Jamal
Bilingual edition (English/ Spanish)
$7

YO SOY #132:
LA LUCHA APENAS COMIENZA
edited by Tania Molina Ramírez
Spanish-language edition
$5

A Dream Foreclosed:
The Great Eviction and the Fight to Live in
America
by Laura Gottesdiener
Available May 1, 2013
$11.95

ZUCCOTTI PARK PRESS
405 61 Street | Brooklyn, New York 11220
occupy@adelantealliance.org
www.zuccottiparkpress.com